PREFACE

I was born in the US and raised on four continents. My mother was from the Mid-West and my father was from the Middle East. My first memories were of Disneyland then soon afterwards Cairo, Egypt and after three years there we moved to Lebanon for a year before spending four years in Baghdad. There was an attempted coup in Iraq in 1967 but I remember in 1968 the Mig jet screaming just above our street as it used it to line up for its assault upon the blue domed Presidential Palace immediately across the Tigris River from our home. That day held many bizarre memories for me including answering the phone during the over-throw. Now the first thing that is usually targeted in an overthrow is the communications that is the telephone, TV, radio so it was a real surprise when the phone rang. I answered and it was my uncle General Assaf. He was the head of the Police of Baghdad, equivalent to the old Garrison of Rome so any overthrow had to have his 'blessing'. "Baba mojude?" (Your dad home?) He asked as he proudly explained that he had just taken the radio station. "Daqeeqa" (just a minute)... 'Hey Dad... you got a phone call... Five Generals and one Colonel (the colonel was Saddam Hussain) took control of the country. But a few weeks afterwards we got another call from General Assaf and there was a hit list going out the next day and my dad's name was on the top of it. At the time my father was a contractor, putting in the sewers of a large part of Baghdad. I knew his father had been Prime Minister of Iraq in the late '50's (Saleh Saad Jabr) but I didn't know at the time that some of the elements in the new regime felt my dad a threat. The next morning my mother, my brothers and myself left Iraq with what we could carry.

Years later, my father began 'representing' the English defense companies that Adnan Kashshogi had once been the agent for in Saudi Arabia before Adnan had the Lockheed bribery scandal. As I shuttled back and forth to Geneva to keep the books of the most sensitive transactions I gained an insight into the workings of one of the three people that ruled Saudi Arabia. After my father made his fortune he began a public campaign against Saddam Hussain in earnest beginning in the early '80's. He announced his political party against Saddam in the House of Parliament in London and in the years that followed it gave me the opportunity to meet some savory and not so savory characters that professed that they wanted to be part of the movement against Saddam. The family consultancy business had quickly expanded into 60 companies in the US, Europe and the Middle East with interests in banking, shipping, computer software, engineering and a myriad of other fields. During this era Saddam had many of his adversaries assassinated, tortured or just disappear. Saddam had made at least two serious assassination attempts on my father, one in London and one in the US as my father's rebellious efforts had gained momentum. Again, I was afforded the opportunity to gain insight into the workings of the US and UK governments as pertaining to Saddam. I learned of loyalty, treachery, pain and suffering and new dimensions of lies, propaganda and hidden agendas. It must be apparent, at the very least understandable, why I have always maintained close ties to Middle Eastern affairs and keen interest to the transpirations in Iraq. Now, after two wars with Iraq, Saddam executed and a US occupation coming to an end there are new enemies to peace in the Middle East, and therefore to global peace.

I believe that the sides have already been chosen and will soon become apparent to the many that have been cuddled and comforted, stirred and stroked by the media bias, propaganda and outright lies propagated by both sides of this Middle East/Western World divide.   I also believe that past political events, associations, sympathies and existing loyalties means that the showdown between Middle East and West will result in World War III and the Coming Jihad. Any 'Peace Negotiations' or other settlement talks between Israel and the Palestinians that could seem to possibly bear any fruit just smacks of the old Biblical Prophesies of the 'False Peace' as fuzzy as those prophesies may be.   The only real question is the "Who, When, Where, Why and How?" of it happening. "World War III and the Coming Jihad" is my explanation of those very issues.

THE COMING JIHAD

There will be World War III in conjunction with a Jihad. Israel and Iran are the principal instigators. It will begin in earnest when the US strikes a blow or it seems imminent that it is about to strike at the Iranian nuclear program or Iran breaks out of its forced containment. This will not be a strike at a single facility as Iran has intentionally separated its nuclear program into many scores of locations with many facilities duplicating critical activity. And to leave Iran's military intact after such a strike would just invite their immediate military retaliation so the most critical elements of the Iranian military structure will also be targeted. In the light of the current political climate this scenario seems plausible, possible and even probable. Of course it can easily be argued that it will not happen, or that the same desired effect can be obtained by employing a comprehensive blockade, or that Iran will allow its nuclear program to be monitored. The problem with painting such a peaceful scenario is that the Jihad has already quietly begun. You may ask does the US really have to resort to military action? Or if the US strikes Iran then what would be the targets? Would the targets have to include military sites and infrastructure? So what if Iran produces 'the bomb'. The questions surrounding this scenario are many and the possible answers number even more.

The reality is that in this play there are several thousand characters, each with a role to perform before the curtain falls. There are Heads of State, religious leaders, politicians and diplomats. There are leaders of countries, generals, spies, scientists, profiteers, media and military industry executives. This massive cast of thousands stands on the shoulders of the thousands that came before them. History of the past half century has embedded an irreparable divide between Israel and the rest of the Middle East. It might be argued that the outcome of the interaction of all these characters cannot be calculated and to attempt to do so with any degree of certainty is impossible. Yet events have already transpired that demand that World War III and the coming Jihad affix itself firmly in our destiny.

Most of these events have been hidden in plain sight, shrouded in bias, propaganda and misinformation. For most people, for both the West and the East, the simple act of even acknowledging these events will be offensive and run counter to all that they have been taught. But no matter how offended one may become it does not change the fact that what has already transpired cannot be changed and that World War III and the coming Jihad is now inevitable.

Iran is a key player. It is important for only one reason, its nuclear program. There is little doubt in anyone's mind that Iran is after 'the bomb'. They have raw uranium in the ground and the oil revenues from 3 million b/d to an oil thirsty world to refine the uranium. In short, they have all the raw material they need and have publicly stated that they have thousands of centrifuges cascading the raw ore towards concentrations necessary for a chain reaction. And of most importance, they have an intense desire to join the Nuclear Club and that, as we have all been told, would be very bad.

The Nuclear Club is not very bad in its own right. At present, it consists of the US, UK, France, Russia, China, India, Pakistan, Israel and arguably North Korea with perhaps a hand full or two of devices. South Africa produced six nuclear devices but dismantled them and canceled their membership to the Nuclear Club. There have been other countries that have had stockpiles of nuclear weapons such as Ukraine, Belarus and Kazakhstan but each returned the stockpiles to Russia and have no current production program. In the past, members of the Nuclear Club have only threatened each other with their respective arsenals but none have dared to use a device in time of war. That is all have dared not, except the US during World War II. But if Iran were to produce nukes it is the consensus that they might indeed use them in a war against Israel. Even with a guaranteed all out nuclear retaliation that would turn Iran into a flat, radioactive sheet of glass, it is totally out of the question to allow Iran nuclear capability. But, again, Iran has the raw materials, the where with all and the intention to join 'The Club', so it's only a matter of time, unless some external force stops them.

Israel fears a nuclear Iran for one simple reason. A nuclear Iran would force Israel to do the unthinkable, and that is to give back some if not all the lands that they took from the Palestinians and other Arabs. There is not a power on Earth that could make Israel revert back to the pre-1967 boarders acceptable to the Palestinians…yet. A nuclear Iran would change that. In this 'scenario', a nuclear Iran forces Israel to give back just some of the land they took from the Arabs, a goal attempted for half a century through wars and peace treaties to no avail. In doing so Iran would take charge of the Islamic World. Those Moslem countries that did not voluntarily follow Iran would face immediate revolution from the masses within. Virtually overnight Iran would have absolute control of 80% of the world's exported oil, which equates to approximately one third of the total world oil consumption. That sounds like a wonderful prospect… to Iran, but to no one else. Certainly not to the fragile kingdoms and dictatorships that constitute the Middle East. Its certain not an appealing situation for oil dependant Europe, Japan and the US. And certainly not acceptable to Israel. Israel would rather go to war than to allow a nuclear Iran dictate one inch of Israeli boarders.

The US will carry out the strikes against Iran on behalf of Israel because it has, for the past few decades, enforced Israeli policy in the Middle East. I would expect some sort of 'revelation' such as a stolen Iranian laptop, a defector, satellite intelligence or other surprising data that 'proves' Iran is after the bomb. The US President will probably first issue ultimatums to Iran that will be totally unacceptable. These may be something along the lines of immediately cease all nuclear production activity and allow total unfettered access by inspectors (US chosen inspectors) anywhere in the country at any time to the total satisfaction of the US, and if the Iranians mobilize their military it will be deemed an act of war. Saddam played along with similar demands for a while in the search for the WMD's then made a mockery of the effort.

Iran may play through such demands going through the motions of compliance or it may not. In any event, the US will unleash a strike to a somewhat prepared Iran. The US will target Iran's known nuclear facilities and attempt to eliminate Iran's capacity to retaliate. Iran has intentionally buried some of its nuclear facilities beneath civilian populated areas. Guaranteed destruction of these known facilities would also guarantee civilian deaths by the thousands. Eliminating, or at the very least greatly reducing Iran's military capacity to retaliate is an absolute necessity in light of the fact that all the US military personnel in Iraq, the Gulf and Afghanistan will be within range of Iran's military and a third of the world's oil production is 'next door', again within striking distance of Iran's missiles, jet fighters, navy and suicide bombers. It should be noted that it is the very slightest of possibilities that Iran is engaged in the largest ruse since the 'Trojan Horse' in that it is not actually developing nuclear warheads but rather going through the exact motions of a concealed program in an effort to trick Israel and the US into attacking. Iran has watched the US lose almost all credibility domestically and in the international community as the search for WMD's in Iraq proved fruitless. If Iran's nuclear program is a ruse then Iran is adept enough to play the sympathy card to their Middle East audience, after the attack and subsequent search, to anger the Moslem population into action against the US. Whether a ruse or not, the US will attack Iran.

As Iran continues to race toward their nuclear goals the window of opportunity to strike Iran before they achieve serious production capability is closing. I'm sure that Israel is sending the US President and every other world leader that they can influence 'post-it' notes to the same effect every day. Such a strike would last a few days and military prudence dictates that it should include every Iranian military asset of any consequence that could be used in retaliation against US and oil interests in the region. The US is capable of tracking and targeting every aircraft, military or other and even destroying those that would be protected under hardened hangers. The US is able to take out almost all of Iran's large missiles capable of reaching Israel, even those on mobile launch platforms. But to eliminate Iran's ability to wreck havoc in the oil fields of the Gulf region, the US would also have to destroy all of the thousands of smaller missiles that can be easily hidden from satellites. And, within each Gulf States and Middle East countries there exists networks of Iranian loyalists ready to wreck havoc and destruction. These networks total several thousand trained and financed individuals many of which are ready for a suicide mission.

During the Iraq/Iran War Iran sent wave after wave of young boys into minefields to clear the path for their more seasoned fighters. Iran is certainly capable of sending wave after wave of little speed boats armed with RPG toting diehards against the thousands of oil derricks, terminals and other flammable installations that dot the Gulf. Iran will strike back. There is a distinct possibility that the counter attack will be of such a nature that would require full US and European engagement, and possibly affording the US President the opportunity to rule over the US while Congress is dissolved and elections postponed as would be expected during a world war.

The oil facilities in the Gulf are the obvious target for Iran's attack or counter attack. Iran will recruit the more radical Arab states to the 'Jihad' including Libya. Iran's retaliation will also include unconventional tactics and be directed at Southern Europe. This is how World War III and the Jihad most probably begin. Israel has long sought a US war with Iran to reduce Iran's military capability and perhaps force a regime change. Iran has been intentionally goading the US and Israel as it makes its play for control of the Moslem World. And the US military industry is still in high gear with the Iraq and Afghan wars and would love to see an Iranian instigated escalation of hostilities. It seems that each of the major participants want this war for their own reasons.

As distasteful as the prospects of this scenario may seem, again, events have already transpired that, I believe, makes this war inevitable. World War III and the Jihad are now our destiny.

In addressing this subject many will be offended, insulted and possibly even shocked. Every person has opinions, particularly about any topic related to Israel. Try to talk in support of Israel in the Middle East and you will be shot down. Try to talk against Israel in the US and you will be shot down. Most people on each side of the Middle East/ Western world divide have no idea the deep level to which they have been conditioned by their respective propaganda. This is easily demonstrated by comparing the following two statements:

"For decades the Israeli government has illegally stolen Arab land, falsely imprisoned and tortured tens of thousands of Arab men, women and children, killed thousands of innocent civilians and murdered those Arabs that they deem a threat to their country without trial or due process of law."

"For decades anti-Israeli Arabs have used kidnapping, assassination, suicide bombers and fired missiles intentionally targeting innocent civilians including women and children for maximum terror effect. They have even attempted the use of chemical agents against the general population."

Most people take offense to one or the other of these statements as lies or propaganda. The reality is that both these statements are absolutely true and worse, much worse. Israel may have been created 'overnight' but the current Middle East predicament has evolve over the past 60 years with atrocity answered with atrocity, propaganda countered with propaganda until there are now two camps in extreme opposition to each other with no way to retreat. It stands upon the lives of tens of thousands of casualties, mostly Arab and the pain and hatred that come with any loss of life. Each side in this conflict has gone to great length to defend their position and discredit the opposition's claim to legitimacy within their respective base of support. Many billions of dollars and countless man hours have been employed by each side to convince and maintain their respective base of support. Fear, hatred, lies, propaganda, orchestrated media campaigns, imprisonment, torture and assassinations have been used by both sides to ensure that their enemy is believed to be the Devil reincarnate. But it is no longer just an Israeli/Palestinian issue, but one that tightly grips the US, most of the Moslem World and much of Europe and Russia. What happens next in the Middle East affects the entire world.

Wars are not just fought on the battlefield but in the hearts and minds of those people behind the fight. Wars go a lot better if there is strong support within the general population base. Support for a war by a general population can be translated into battlefield weapons and political power can often be more effective than any tank or jet.

Political power can garner support from other countries in the form of financial or military aid, embargoes, sanctions or even blockades. Inversely, a lack of support can spell defeat exemplified by the case of the US in Viet Nam or the Soviet Union in Afghanistan. The need to develop or nurture support can vary greatly. In the case of the US entering WWII the need was miniscule following the attack on Pearl Harbor. Generally speaking, the less just an offensive is, the more need there is to 'influence' public opinion to the contrary.

How important is public opinion in the Middle East conflict? It has been the weapon most employed by far and is responsible for the decades of protraction without resolution. The arsenal in the 'War on Opinion' begins with the mainstream media such as Television, radio, newspapers and magazines. The News is obviously of primary importance. It is not just controlling what is reported but how it is reported that makes the difference. To illustrate this point, recently Iranian President Ahmadinajad was invited to speak at Columbia University where he attempted to bring to light the Middle East perspective on the Palestinian issue. He mentioned that whatever happened to the Jews during WWII happened in Europe and not in Palestine yet the Palestinians have had to suffer for it for the past sixty years. In the days that followed his speech most all of the coverage in the US media centered around the Iranian president's denial that there are gays in Iran. To address anything other than his statement regarding gays in Iran would bring to light the genuine injustice done to the Palestinians and cast doubt on the Israeli treatment of the same. This is just one simple example of the thousands and thousands of bias reporting of Pro-Israeli/Anti-Arab events over the past few years. It was poor reporting, bias and of very little value except as another example of the pro-Israeli lobby working to influence American public opinion. Beyond the 'news' there are editorials, articles, and general entertainment shows that all contribute to the opinion making process. Total and absolute control of the mainstream media is the primary objective if a campaign to influence the minds and hearts is to succeed. Both camps in the Middle East conflict have achieved this milestone in their respective markets many years back.

In the Arab countries and Iran, each country has established effective control over all elements of their mainstream media (the internet and satellite being relatively new and somewhat of the exceptions). Each country may have its own unique twist to the control but control they have. All allow the unfettered bashing of Israel and disallow any sympathetic or even neutral views on the issue. Negative rumors regarding Israeli atrocities are also allowed. Some of the countries that their governments have close dealings with the US may tone down some of the official rhetoric but for the most part the hatred of Israel is kept alive. In the case of Israel they have focused most of their efforts towards the US and have long established effective control over the

US mainstream media. They have significant influence in much of the Western European media but by no means exercise the total dominance as in the US.

The battles in the political arena are fought in totally different ways. In this battlefield Israel has won the American ground and with it, the annual contribution of tens of billions of dollars worth of the most advanced military hardware available and the protection of the US veto power over the UN that keeps Israel censure free. It has taken Israel years of painstaking diligence to achieve this victory over the US with an effective shutout of Arab influence. Broadcast television and especially broadcast news has been totally compromised. Critical mass of support has also been achieved in the US press and radio. If any US politician or candidate does not actively exhibit or declare their pro-Israeli sentiments then they can expect a full frontal assault on every television set in America until they publicly change their position or have to withdraw from politics. Not one single Congressman has challenged the Israeli lobby and their political careers remain unscathed after being labeled as an anti-Semite. This political pressure extends into the White House, as most US Presidents don't even bother to publicly challenge Israel even if Israeli ambitions conflict with US interests. President George W. Bush never met with the only truly democratically elected Arab leader during his entire first term in office because that man was Yassir Arafat, the duly elected leader of the National Palestinian Authority. For years the National Palestinian Authority has never been referred to with 'National' in its title in the US press but only as the 'Palestinian Authority'. That is like referring to the United States of America as the 'States of America'. The reason 'National' is omitted when referring to the National Palestinian Authority seems to be to eliminate any since of a Palestinian nation. That all the mainstream US media participates in this distortion is another indication as to the great lengths the propaganda war is waged.

The Administration also relies heavily upon the input of the State Department's Near East Affairs division. This is the area of the government that has been the focus of Israel's efforts to influence US Middle East policy. It is dominated by Jews and very pro-Israeli non-Jews so that all policies concerning the Middle East just happen to be in the direct interest of Israel. This lock on the US Congress and Administration comes with an automatic veto of any UN resolution that is detrimental to Israel. The US is a permanent member of the UN Security Council and has vetoed scores of United Nations General Assembly resolutions condemning Israel for everything from human rights violations to illegal land grabs to atrocities just short of genocide against the Palestinians. No sanctions, no condemnations, no nothing detrimental in any way to Israel passes by the US veto in the UN. As a general rule these vetoes are never reported in the US mainstream media. The US just does not tolerate anti-Semitic reporting in any fashion. The US blindly supports Israel to such a degree that there is no reporting of any event or Israeli activity that shows Israel in anything less than the righteous underdog. In the US it is Israel not the Middle East that has won the propaganda war. The Arab world doesn't stand a chance to break the Israeli lock on the US. The most that the Arab lobby can achieve is to have some of the vernacular changed so that 'Arab' and 'Terrorist' are no longer synonymous but gets replaced with 'Islamic extremists' or 'Jihadists'.

The Middle East failure to gain a footing in the battle for US propaganda rights is due to a number of factors. First and foremost is because of the nature of Middle East politics, a term that is somewhat of an oxymoron when applied to the Arab world. Most of the Middle East countries are ruled by dictatorships or monarchies of sorts, all very fragile in their rule. Most are preoccupied with their own survival and power retention. And most, not all, are concerned with their 'retirement plans', that is skimming off as much money as they can. There are the exceptions such as Iran, a non-Arab state ruled by a cleric (the Supreme Leader) and a handful of his religious followers. Lebanon too is an exception to this pattern, however, it has been consumed by a lengthy Christian/Moslem civil war followed by its occupation by Syria until recently. Lebanon has its hands too full wrenching and maintaining control from various international interests to be concerned with someone else's problems. Most of the Middle Eastern countries are ruled by a few score 'haves' atop a powder keg of 'have not's' relatively speaking, each with absolute control over the media in country. In short, each are primarily concerned with solidifying their power for their own survival and after that, the lining of their own pockets. One does not talk badly about the Saudi monarchy or ruling clique while in Saudi Arabia for fear of that one-way helicopter ride over the Rub-Al Khali desert. Mean while, they continue to stash double digit billions of dollars in their foreign accounts skimmed from every major contract transacted with their country. Several of these kingdoms or sheikdoms have created a parliament which is little more than a show piece that acts in an advisory capacity to the ruler. But this is the way that governments are run in the Middle East. This is the way that business is conducted. The masses throughout the Middle East have been fed a steady diet of hate and revenge for decades and there is no undoing those teachings over night. If efforts to reverse this propaganda were to begin immediately it would take at least one if not two generations for this hatred to diminish. Though the ruling elite may like to see the destruction of Israel and the establishment of a Palestinian state it is the brainwashed masses that are the real danger. When a serious challenge to the power of Israel shows itself it is the masses that will gather around in support of such efforts and woe be the fragile monarchy that tries to dampen or ignore the 'Calling'.
There has been so much propaganda on both sides of the issue that Iran can now take advantage of this and the reigning dictators and monarchs will have little choice but to try to hold on as they ride the whirlwind. This is the danger of having been subject to decades of propaganda. In the short run the propagandists, both East and West, believe that they are furthering their cause and combating the effects of the opposition's propaganda while in reality they have forced the choosing of sides based up half truths and outright lies that leaves war as the only option to resolve the differences.

The very nature of political power in today's world is based upon lies and distortions. If the truths be known then there would be no Israeli injustice towards the Palestinians because there would be a Palestine. There would no longer be the dictatorships and monarchies that govern most of the Middle East and the American administration would have to reflect the desires of an informed voting public. America now knows that, at the very least, President George W. Bush gravely distorted the truth that was presented to the American people to gain support for the occupation of Iraq. It is becoming increasingly evident that Iraq had become a pretense to redistribute hundreds of billions of present and future US tax dollars into the hands of the military industry. Such was the deception regarding Iraq, but in the case of the US attacking Iran, the motivation is not primarily for money or oil, but for the concerns and ambitions of Israel.

One can look at any situation and twist and distort the perceptions until it has nothing to do with reality, well someone's reality. Let me illustrate using something that most of us are familiar with, Dorothy and the Wizard of Oz. We all know that Dorothy was a sweet, innocent, loving Mid-Western girl that loved her little dog too. But the propaganda from the 'Evil Witches Guild of Oz' paints a totally different story. Dorothy had trained her beast to terrorize and attack the innocent citizens of Kansas; in particular a poor, little old lady that was so poor she had to ride a bicycle. When the authorities issued a warrant for the capture of the beast, Dorothy and her dog became fugitives from the law and fled to Oz. The first thing that Dorothy did when she went to Oz was to murder a little old lady in cold blood, a little old lady that never did her any harm. Then before the old lady was even cold Dorothy stole her shoes. She sets off on a Crusade gathering her forces as she goes by lying to them and promising them whatever they want such as a brain for the Scarecrow, a heart for the Tin man and courage for the Lion. She gets stoned in her opium fields of bright red flowers before she continues on her mission. That mission is the genocide of all the 'evil doer' witches of Oz. After she murders the last evil doer she resorts to sorcery to escape back to her homeland. Dorothy therefore is a lying, thieving, murdering merciless fugitive junkie. Facts are facts and open to distortion. The validity of such arguments can always be questioned. The validity of the propaganda on both sides of the current Middle East turmoil should be questioned. It has to be questioned if Peace is sought.

Our history of events in the Middle East has been similarly distorted and now we are on the verge of World War III. The US has cornered Iran because it is a threat to Israel. It is a threat to Israel because Israel has unjustly taken the Palestinian lands, cast them out with nothing and worse. Israel has been allowed to do this because they have gained the support of the American government, media and people. Now Iran can take advantage of the decades of distortions surrounding the Middle East and force a Jihad to elevate it's standing in the Moslem world. America will force Iran to take these desperate actions. It is too late to concern ourselves with 'right' or 'wrong', there is just time enough to figure out how this catastrophe will unfold and to protect ourselves as best we can. It will also be our duty to never let this happen again.

This era is one of great change. Some of these changes have significantly changed the balance of powers. The full impact of these changes has yet to be realized. There are three changes in particular that are major influences to World War III and the coming Jihad. These are the creation of the state of Israel, the use of oil as a global weapon and the battle for leadership of the Moslem world.

The creation of the state of Israel is important in so far as how and where it was created. It was created not by the current residents of the area at the time but by third parties. It displaced Palestinians and they fought back. They lost what lands were left to them. Other Arab countries joined against the Israeli rule only to suffer defeat and more loss of land and again. Other than the humiliation of defeat, the Arabs have lost land even after the return of the Sinai. You may kill an Arab tribal leader then his first son may or may not extract revenge on you, however, if you take his land then that guarantees that there will be war. Israel took Arab land and the Arabs, all Arabs want it back. Because of Israel's brutal and barbaric treatment of the Palestinians it has become the only single unifying issue throughout the entire Middle East.

OPEC raised its head during the October '73 war. The Arab countries that constituted a majority within OPEC (OAPEC- Organization of Arab Petroleum Exporting Countries) threaten an oil embargo against any country that helped Israel during the war. During the first Gulf War oil was used as a weapon of sorts. And now, with an oil thirsty world consuming the total production and refining capacity of the oil producing countries, oil is once again of utmost importance. The vast majority of the worlds exported oil comes from the Persian Gulf and any major disruption of production would undoubtedly cause a near total collapse of the world economy. Even a small disruption would cause an already nervous oil market to spike to levels that would wreck havoc with many economies.

The battle for Islam has begun in earnest. It's roots can be traced back to 1979 with the overthrow of the Shah of Iran by Khomeini. That taking of hostages at the US embassy in Tehran became a convenient campaign target for then presidential candidate Ronald Reagan. The hostages became a focal point for Reagan's campaign to illustrate the ineffectual Carter Administration. Iran was going to return the hostages to Carter but the Reagan camp convinced Iran to keep the hostages until Reagan was elected then they could return the hostages when Reagan was inaugurated and all would be well. The Iranians kept their end of the bargain and returned the hostages as Reagan became president. But, for whatever reason, Reagan continued to use Iran as a whipping post. The rise of an Islamic state also disturbed Iran's neighbors, as they were nothing more than fragile monarchies or dictatorships. When Iran was weakest after their internal 'purification' of Shah supporters, Iraq was encourage to attack and lay claim to the Shatt-Al Arab waterway, the oil rich area of river divide between the two countries. Saddam, a Sunni, used this opportunity to draft many of the angry young Shiites that he had thrown in prison and pit them against the Iranian Shiites on the battlefield. The Gulf countries including Saudi Arabia and the US supported Iraq. Iran suffered greatly during the following eight years of war. It was clear that Iran had many enemies. Now Iran faces a full frontal assault from the US and Israel with no prospect of help from the current governments of most of the Arab countries. Iran will not capitulate to the US and Israel. Capitulation is weakness and if Iran capitulates to others, then they will have to capitulate to the will of their people, most of whom just want to get on with life and enjoy it. So it has become an 'all or nothing' dilemma for Iran. The only way out for Iran is to lead the Moslem World. And a nuclear armed Iran could easily pressure the entire Gulf region and Israel, so that scenario will not be allowed to happen by Israel visa vie the US. The only other way for Iran to lead the Moslem World is to force a Jihad against Israel and the US.

Israel is a thorn in the Middle East side that will not go away. The importance of oil in today's oil thirsty world means that any major conflict in the region puts the entire global economy at risk of total collapse. And with Iran developing nuclear weapons in an effort to lead the Moslem World means that conflict is inevitable. World War III and the coming Jihad approaches.

IRAN

Iran, under the rule of the Shah, maintained close relations with the U.S. The Iranians, not considered Arabs, were a welcomed ally in the region. The Shah became the regional power with the help of the American military. Phantom jets, US training for the pilots and a host of other support gave the Shah the military might to put down any Arab uprising in the Gulf. During the October '73 Arab Israeli war Israel lost one hundred and five fighter aircraft in the first few days of the war. Israel's air force had suffered a tremendous blow and the US had the Shah lend Israel some of its fighter jets until the US could get more support to Israel. The Shah also maintained the largest hover craft fleet in the world, enabling quick response to any situation in the oil rich Gulf. The Shah ruled his country with an iron fist called the SAVAK. During his reign, the Shah and his clique became immensely wealthy. He did try to bring his country into the twentieth century but repressed any challenge to his regime with stern authority. It is estimated that at least one hundred thousand people 'disappeared' under the Shah. And as with any repressive regime in the Middle East, the last vestiges of resistance were in the religious sector. It was from the Mosques that rebellion smoldered and that Khomeini emerged.

Ayatollah Khomeini had been in exile from the Shah's Iran for twelve and a half years in Northern Iraq. He would pass out his 'seditious' anti-Shah literature and conducted his sermons to Iranian pilgrims that would make the trip to Mosul and other Holy Shiite shrines in Iraq. Then, in 1979 Khomeini went to Paris for six months, presumably to meet the people that could advance his career, then road the whirlwind back into Iran. He began his cleansing of all Shah Loyalists, particularly in the military. The few generals and officers that were not executed were thrown in prison.

It was during this turbulent time that the US embassy was taken over and hostages held. That gave rise to ABC's Nightline with Ted Kopple. For the first day and a half of the hostage crisis Ted Kopple was reporting that it was communist students that had over run the embassy and taken the embassy personnel hostage. Indeed, that is how the trouble began. The communist students were desperate and scrambling for their lives. Iran had just been transformed into an extreme Islamic nation that was still purifying itself with executions too many to count. Under that regime you could have been many things and still had survived. You could have been a moderate Moslem, even a Christian or a Jew as written in the Koran and that they must be tolerated. The one thing you could not be was a member of an atheist organization such as the Communist Party. All those communist students presumably came from Moslem households and should therefore be Moslem. There is nothing lower in the Moslem world, absolutely nothing lower than a Moslem that has turned his back on Islam. Islam is supposed to be a one way street. The communist students were on the clock and in an act of desperation for their very survival they took over the US embassy and held hostage its occupants. In one daring move they went from being next on the diabolical inquisition list, with having nothing to bargain for their lives, to forcing a superpower to negotiate with them. The risk of having the captives slaughtered and angering the US further was an untimely prospect for the Ayatollah to say the least. Khomeini had his hands full with trying to consolidate his position and was not adept with Western Politics. For a quick-fix, the Ayatollah had his people surround the embassy with orders that nothing goes in or out without his express permission until he could diffuse and control the situation. This allowed the situation to deteriorate and be transformed into different issues by other international concerns with their own agendas.

Iran's military structure was in ruins and its machinery was grinding to a stop. During this time of low ebb, Saddam Hussein was encouraged to take advantage of Iran's vulnerability and he attacked the oil rich Shatt-Al-Arab waterway. This was the disputed dividing line between Iran and Southern Iraq and was home to much of Iran's oil infrastructure. This was a costly war for Iran in human terms as they were grossly under equipped and untrained, having cleansed their military so thoroughly. During the initial phase of the war Iraq made gains into Iranian territory. During this war it became increasingly apparent that Iran was becoming more hard-line radical as they sacrificed their young teens and preteens to clear the minefields laid out by a retreating Iraq. Iran regained its lost territory and began to advance into Iraq. It was then Saddam used Chemical weapons on the unprepared Iranians and halted their advance. As the war continued for eight years Saddam used the opportunity to extort billions of dollars in financial support from the Gulf States and vast military aid from the US. The Iranian death toll rose to one million or approximately 2% of its population before a cease-fire was implemented. During this war the US increased sanctions against Iran for all military, dual use items and eventually all non-humanitarian goods. The US also supplied Iraq with real time satellite intelligence so that Iraq could timely counter every move made by the Iranians with lethal effects. The CIA organized several billion dollars worth of credit with the US Export/Import Bank through a network of some 165 front companies and banks (Banc de Lavro in particular) for the purchase of US grain. Much of the grain was rerouted during shipment to Eastern European countries in exchange for weapons that were delivered to Iraq. The US attacked Iranian oil facilities in the Gulf and even downed a civilian airliner on a routine flight over the Gulf killing all on board. Iran's list of friends was shortening.

After the war with Iraq, Iran had to adopt different strategies. Iran could no longer afford direct military confrontation with anybody using their inferior Soviet, North Korean and Chinese military hardware. But they had to weaken their enemies or give them something else to worry about. They embarked upon a campaign that bred discontent in the regional countries. The used subterfuge and networked terror cells. They armed insurgents and trained them where possible. All this they did at arm's length for plausible deniability. The Middle East was ripe for these tactics. Under the capable direction of Rafsanjani and others, Iran was able to divert the efforts of the region away from direct confrontation with Iran. It wasn't long before each of these countries faced growing 'domestic' problems that required attention. It became far more economical militarily, politically and financially to conduct this type of warfare. There is the saying "The enemy of my enemy is my friend." Add to that "If my enemy has no enemy then we can make them some.". Supporting and arming (at arm's length) a radical terrorist cell in another Middle East country that goes out and kills a group of tourists causes that country to lose millions of tourism dollars and demands that they spend millions more to combat such activities. Likewise, taking Western hostages generated media coverage and support for their cause that they couldn't otherwise buy. In this war of attrition sponsoring a few hundred short range missiles that reach only a few miles into Israeli occupied territory forces Israel to maintain it's military on heightened alert status and employing vast resources in its military operations and intelligence services in an already stressed economy. Likewise, supplying new and improved IEDs in Iraq has forced the US to first, up-armor the thousands of Humvees, then begin to replace them with entirely new vehicles able to withstand to new assaults. In this particular case the Pentagon had requested between 17,000 and 20,000 Mine Resistant Ambush Protected (MRAPs) vehicles at a cost of over one million dollars each. That's about $20 billion.

Due to the long-standing sanctions, Iran has begun to produce their own weaponry. Now they produce most of their weaponry including medium range missiles and jet fighters. They have put up their own satellite in low orbit and working on a three stage rocket for higher orbits. They still outsource some of their high-end electronic based warfare systems when they can, through Russia primarily. Their military hardware development has been directed towards certain goals that give an indication of what their intentions may be. Their medium range missiles can certainly target Israel; however, if placed in other Arab countries such as Syria or Libya then many European cities could come under threat. The attempts by the US to prevent Iran from acquiring weapons detrimental to Israel or Europe have forced Iran to become somewhat self-sufficient in this regard. Iran can now become a supplier to nations, organizations and groups that would otherwise not consider gaining such military leverage due to the lack of availability. Don't forget that the US has already labeled Syria as an enemy and the US has already tried to kill Khaddafi of Libya instead killing a few members of his family. I believe that Khaddafi maintains a serious grudge against America.

Iran's ultimate objective is to fulfill the Islamic destiny and convert the entire world to Islam, their Islam. They have to pave the way for the 'Mehdi' so he can set about delivering all of us. But first things first. Before they take on the world they must take over or at least lead the Moslem world in a Jihad against Israel and the US. If they were victorious in this endeavor then this would certainly give them immense economic power that could easily be leveraged to cause all sorts of mischief. Approximately one third of the entire world's oil production comes from Moslem countries. That equates to 75%-80% of all exported oil. Russia, Venezuela and Mexico are some of the larger non-Moslem oil exporters. But to unify the Moslem world Iran would have to be able to battle Israel and at the very least force Israel to give the Palestinians a homeland. To force the creation of a genuine Palestinian nation, regardless of the initial size, would give Iran the critical mass of support that they need within each Middle East country to force their allegiance or regime change. An Iran that is even in the midst of a raging battle to deliver a Palestinian nation could easily call on the population of any Middle East country to topple the regime if they don't help. Most of the regimes are fragile monarchies or dictatorships that are run by just a few score of people. For decades the vast majority of the Arab population has been fed large doses of anti-Israeli propaganda. It does not take much to call upon that hatred especially if the call to arms is made after the battle has begun. But for Iran to force Israel to the bargaining table, Iran would need nuclear weapons. There is only one highly improbable reason why Iran will not actually develop nuclear weapons and that is if they just want to draw the US out in a ruse. If Iran can make Israel and the US believe that it is developing nuclear weapons then it invites attack. If the US attacks Iran and no trace of Weapons of Mass Destruction are found by subsequent UN inspection teams then the US loses all credibility in the Middle East and would face demands by popular uprising for their ejection. But it is more than fair to assume that Iran will stop at nothing to refine the raw uranium that they have in the ground into weapons grade purity. Raw ore can start at 0.7% purity, then you need to separate the U235 from the U238 by centrifuging it in hexafluoride gas. Iran is somewhere near the 20% purity while you need 90% purity or better for the big bang. However, to reach the 20% purity takes 90% of the effort and continued cascading of the 20% purity becomes easier and easier towards the weapons grade material. Iran wants to produce its own nuclear weapons and lots of them. To have one or two weapons says volumes, however, to be able to produce about a hundred weapons to rival Israel's arsenal would mean Iran could force Israel to the Palestinian homeland bargaining table. Iran could even supply nuclear weapons to the Moslem countries that follow its lead.

It is highly probable that Iran already has purchased or made at least one low yield nuclear weapon or at the very least very close to making one. The whirlwind begins in Iran. It has already begun.

ISRAEL

The birth of Israel could be described as a Cesarean birth without anesthetics. It was born out of the atrocities the Jews in Europe suffered under Hitler. After World War II fragments of what is now Israel were carved out for Jewish rule and fragments were set aside for the Palestinian. This did not sit well for the local Palestinian population directly affected and there was armed rebellion against the new decrees. To make a long story short, Israel ended up with all the land in question. Israel had to fight for its inception and to fight for survival ever since. And it has acquired a little bit more land along the way.

In 1967 the Arabs posed a somewhat unified front to challenge Israel. The Arabs were armed with inferior Soviet weapons but outnumbered the Israelis. The Arabs suffered a humiliating defeat and lost substantial land, including the Sinai Peninsula, the West Bank and the Golan Heights.

The next time Israel faced a unified Arab threat was in October 1973. This time they faced new tactics and newer Soviet weapons and the use of an oil embargo. The Israelis were able to fend off advances along the Syrian border as they had detailed intelligence of almost every Syrian gun placements. The Israelis had constructed the Bar-Lev line along the Suez Canal as a barrier to halt the advance of any Egyptian armor. But Egypt had suffered several years of poor economy that drove many university students into the military. Among the new recruits were plenty of engineering students that were capable of operating the water cannons used to wash down the giant man-made sand dunes of the Bar-Lev line. The Egyptians washed away the sand dunes here and there and threw up temporary bridges to roll their armor into the Sinai. The Israeli Air Force tried desperately to destroy the bridges but the Egyptians would throw up new ones. The Israeli aircraft were decimated when they tried to stop the advancing armored as they had to cross through the kill-zones of SAM 6&7 missile batteries. These missiles worked well in the open flat desert terrain and downed 100 Israeli aircraft and another 5 aircraft were downed by radar guided cannon. The Israelis sent their tanks to engage the Egyptian tanks only to be met by the Egyptian infantry using TOW wire guided missiles. This is the first time that infantry took on tanks and won. The Egyptians were employing tactics that the Israelis could not combat. There was nothing to stop the Egyptians from advancing into the heart of Israel. In a desperate and courageous effort the Israelis sent a task force that re-crossed the Suez Canal and cut off the Egyptian 2nd army. The Egyptian army was poised to destroy the Israeli task force when President Sadat allowed a cease-fire and negotiated peace. Sadat was almost ousted by his generals at the time but he knew that if he continued with their advance on Israel then Israel would use their nuclear weapons. The oil embargo by the Arab states within OPEC showed Israel that the US was the only country able to pull through for them in a crunch. Most of the highly oil dependent European countries had to capitulate to the 'hands off' demands of the embargo or face being cut off. The US even had difficulty finding a European country that would allow their planes of support for Israel to land and refuel. Portugal allowed such rights, probably from their long standing dislike of the Arabs.

In between and after these wars, Israel has had to face the growing tide of guerilla attacks, suicide bombers and of late, small missiles lobed onto them from areas in Southern Lebanon and the Gaza Strip. Israel knows war. Man for man it certainly has one of the best militaries in the world. It knows how to defend and how to attack. But sadly, Israel does not know peace. It does not know how to make or keep peace. The one leader that they had that made peace with the Egyptians was assassinated.

Israel receives huge amounts of aid from the US. Much of the aid is in the form of military gifts. There are official US figures that show sales of military hardware and service to Israel. There are also huge amounts of 'unofficial' support that they receive that are not reported as such to government agencies. Perhaps the Israelis are sensitive to the amount of aid that they receive from the US government or the US government is sensitive about the same. In short, they receive more than ten times the amount of aid per capita than the next highest US aid recipient. Israel receives more military aid from the US than all the other recipients of US military aid combined. If the US did not give Israel such vast amounts of aid then Israel would have long ago had to make peace. But Israel needs this aid because it is surrounded by countries that have made war on it several times. Everyone seems to hate them in their part of the world. It's not just their immediate neighbors either. They are despised along a 5,000-mile band from Morocco to Pakistan. This is the reality of their neighborhood. It is good that America is their friend because the United Nation General Assembly has passed resolution after resolution condemning Israel for its actions only to fall prey to the US veto in the Security Council. Typical votes in the General Assembly against Israel unfold with a few dozen mostly America's European allies abstaining from the vote, America, Israel and half a dozen Pacific Island nations under US influence vote against the resolution and the rest of the world votes to pass the condemnation of Israel. This pattern has been repeated so many times that President G. W. Bush has called on the United Nations to stop picking on Israel and turn their attention to other violators of human rights.

As tensions mount in the Middle East, Israel will seem to attempt to diffuse the situation with peace talks with the Palestinians. Agreements may be within reach and even signed but there will be no peace in the Middle East. Whatever peace deals may happen all will be negated when it is evident that war is inevitable. Israel will not go back to pre-1967 boarders and leave all their settlements that they built in the West Bank. They want every drop of precious water that they now control and certainly don't want to share it with the millions of Palestinian refugees that would flock to a homeland of their own. And to have an independent Palestinian nation of millions with their own military right next door after the way they have mistreated the Palestinians for decades would be suicidal. And Israel will never relinquish control of Jerusalem, never again. They have made their bed and now they have to lie in it, unfortunately they have maneuvered the US is into the same bed.

Most of the American public views Israel in a very favorable light. That is the only light in which Israel has been shown in the US. Most have been shielded from the opinions of the United Nation and the 'cooperation' of US and Israel on Middle East policy. Most of the US population has no idea what is the real root cause for the Middle East hatred of Israel and now the same hatred that is extended to the US. For years the US broadcast support for Israel. Anybody that attempts to deviate from this total unconditional support for Israel is immediately label as anti-Semitic and pressured into oblivion. The real sin here is that the pro-Israeli lobby believes that it is doing a great service to Israel when in reality they have enabled Israel to abuse the great power it has obtained from the US and give rise to the hatred that will definitely be the cause of World War III and pretty much the annihilation of Israel as it stands today. Simply put, if America did not blindly support Israel with vast amounts of the highest tech weaponry and protect it from international censure, then Israel would have had to long ago come to some amicable relationship with the displaced Palestinians. Israel will not budge, it will not give the Palestinians a meaningful homeland. World War III begins and ends in Israel. It has begun.

UNITED STATES

The administration of George W. Bush was definitely 'big-business friendly'. With the War on Terror, the Iraq War, the Afghanistan War and the looming War with Iran, the military industrial complex, of which President Eisenhower warned, profited greatly. Hundreds of billions of new dollars flowed through their accounts under the most favorable terms. No-competition bids, cost-plus contracts and only the slightest façade of oversight. Oil had enjoyed record returns as well in an Administration friendly environment. The global oil industry was pumping and refining near absolute capacity with no checks on consumption short of some European countries imposing relatively higher gas taxes. The price of crude oil soared to over $120 a barrel with the US consuming about a quarter of the worlds production.

It seems that the more regulated a big business was, then the more influence they could exert on the G. W. Bush Administration such as the pharmaceutical, medical and insurance industries, as oil was already a 'shoe-in'. A second characteristic of the 'W' Administration was their philosophy of big business can do a better job than big government in areas of education and social security with attempts to introduce tuition vouchers and changes in investment regulations for individual social security accounts. Many Americans agreed with this Administration's philosophy towards big business and government and many Americans disagreed with the same. It is highlighted here not to condone or condemn but to identify it as having been a factor of some barring in the US policy in the Middle East and in particular with regards to Iraq.

That Administration had its own agenda for growing the military might of the US. It had also put in safeguards to insulate itself from the population concerned with America's coarse. The Administration had total power over the individual without regard to any civil rights or judicial process. These powers are in place but to date no widespread use or misuse has occurred. There have been cases where individuals have been detained and even tortured without regard to America's perceived inalienable rights, but again, no widespread misuse has occurred. Effectively after the 'Patriot Act' the US Administration had the power to do whatever they wanted and the ability to challenge any opposition overtly or covertly. The public would better tolerate the widespread use of these dictatorial powers if there were a genuine threat to our country as in the time of a world war, instead of just a declared war on terror. This would be particularly true if the war was with an enemy that could destroy much of the oil that keeps this world turning and strike terror in the hearts of the general population with delivery capabilities of Weapons of Mass Destruction. Any Presidency faced with such an enemy could use dictatorial powers to combat an enemy with the speed and ferocity that is required and could possibly implement some social, economic and legal changes along the way.

It is not coincidence that the coming war with Iran is precisely what Israel wants. It is the reason that the war is coming. If Israel were to attack Iran then it risks unifying the entire Middle East in armed retaliation. But if the US were to save the world from a nuclear Iran after years of attempting non-military solutions, then the world could be made to accept that action. For years now the US and Israel have been increasing their antagonist rhetoric against Iran in preparing the populations for the inevitable. In the past few years the propaganda machine has been working increasingly harder to prepare the US for the coming war. War with Iran has been openly discussed in the US media to a degree that includes tactics and targets. It is not the US military that is initiating the calls to strike Iran. The pro-Israeli lobby has the mechanisms in place to 'encourage' favorable articles towards its ends. The lobby can also pressure many politicians and has extensive influence within the State Department, particular the Near East division responsible for Arab Israeli affairs.

For the past few decades Israel has exerted near total dominance within the Near East division. Pro-Israeli sympathizers within the Near East division control much, if not all, the information flow upon which policy and strategic decisions are based. This has lead to blunders in the US foreign policy particularly in assessing or dealing with the Palestinians. For example, during the entire first term of George W. Bush there was only one genuinely democratically elected Arab leader and the US President refused to meet with him. The only democratically elected Arab happened to be Yassir Arafat, the Palestinian who spent his entire adult life fighting for a homeland for his people while avoiding assassination attempts by Israel. Arafat's adversary was the Israeli hardliners and during the many years that Arafat's diplomatic efforts fell upon deaf ears he lead the military campaign against Israel. There was no way that Israel would want to deal with Arafat as a head of state, duly elected or not. After Arafat's death it was evident that the Palestinians were at the crossroads.

President Bush must have had the idea in his head from somewhere that the Hamas were just a handful of militant radicals that just kept exploding bombs in Israel and firing scores of little rockets into the same. That was before he endorsed and pushed for a Palestinian election that would democratically elect a government that could finally negotiate with Israel for a permanent peace. What the Near East division of the State Department presumably failed to inform the President was that Hamas was also responsible for setting up many free clinics and free schools for the children that would otherwise have none. And Hamas was still a champion of the Palestinian struggle for a homeland, carrying on the battle against Israel with suicide bombings, rocket attacks and other tactics that forced Israel to divert their resources from economic enterprises to military ones. Perhaps naively the President thought that elections would cast Hamas into oblivion and give Bush the pretense to ignore or even target Hamas. Advice from some Arab countries to the contrary was ignored. So on January 26th, 2006 the Palestinian Legislative Council elections were held. Hamas won 74 out of the 132 seats or 56% of the council. On March 29th, 2006 the Hamas 24 member cabinet was sworn in the Palestinian National Authority. It quickly became clear that Israel and the US rejected the election on the grounds that they just didn't like the winner and would not deal with the duly elected Hamas. The US quickly branded Hamas as a 'Terrorist Organization' to discredit and disqualify the election results. Perhaps the Bush/Cheney Administration thought it wise or in Israel's interest to make back-channel ultimatums, conditions and inducements to the Palestinian party heads but soon thereafter intra-Palestinian fighting broke out between the newly elected Hamas and the outgoing Fatah party. It wasn't until March 2007 that a National Unity Government was formed amongst Hamas, Fatah and the independents and was headed by Prime Minister Haniya (Hamas). But the fighting continued to escalate with kidnappings and murders in June and Hamas took full control of Gaza. President Abbas dissolved the National Unity Government and declared a state of emergency appointing a Government headed by Salam Fayyad and made up of Fatah members and Independents, with Hamas members nowhere to be found.

If there is to be any real and lasting peace that creates a Palestinian state on the West Bank then America has to be responsible and not the Iranians. By putting in place a process by which a Palestine seems possible, the US can greatly reduce the motivation of Iran to deliver the same. There will be no peace so long as the US Administration continues to support Israel without question. That kind of support means that Israel can leave the negotiating table at any time with impunity. For propaganda purposes Israel may want to sit at the table but negotiations can easily be drawn out for months or years while 'progress' is being made.

When the second Bush Administration decided to invade Iraq it genuinely surprised Israel. Not so much the decision to invade, but the timing of the invasion. Of course Saddam was on Israel's enemy list but less pressing than Iran that has held first place for some years now. Iraq seemed too tempting a target for President Bush to ignore. All the fundamentals seemed perfect and indeed, most were. Iraq was ruled by one of the most repressive psychopaths of the twentieth century. Saddam was hated and feared by Iraq's neighbors, including and especially by Iran. A freed Iraqi people should be grateful to America. America had already engaged Iraqi troops over the first Gulf War and proved our weapons and tactics were far superior. Communications with sitting Iraqi Generals just prior to the onset of the war indicated that with a little help from the US, elements within the Iraqi Army could seize control away from Saddam. Apparently even Saddam was willing to go into self-imposed exile for a billion dollars to add to his fortune. And Iraq is strategically located between Iran and Israel, offering the US a land based front to halt any ambitions that Iran may have on its way to Israel. An American military presence in Iraq would also keep Syria in check as Iraq shares a long border with Syria. Iraq has oil and lots of it, perhaps as much as Saudi Arabia. Plenty of wealth for a grateful and free Iraq to share with its liberators. The US could easily estimate locking up about $300 billion dollars in mostly oil servicing contracts. The US was willing to share the coming financial bonanza with its partner, the UK, based roughly upon their level of participation of about 20%.

Saddam was one of the most barbaric tyrants in modern history. He used chemical weapons of mass destruction killing thousands of Kurds and Iranian soldiers. He had biological weapons and the ability to strike Israel. When President Bush ousted Saddam, the world should have been grateful. Ousting Saddam was fairly easy as most Iraqis hated their dictator. Installing a sympathetic government was easy as Iraq was eager to embrace liberty. But the miscalculations and outright blunders that followed prevented America from fast tracking the rebuilding contracts. The Bush/Cheney Administration was certainly expecting lucrative contracts from the Iraqi oil industry. Iraq would need everything from refineries and massive refurbishing of its oil facilities to ongoing maintenance of their wells, pipeline network and terminals. It did not happen as planned.

But to measure the success or failure of the Iraq campaign one must first clearly identify the objectives. For example, if the objective of the US action in Iraq was to simply remove Saddam then we could say 'mission accomplished'. Again, if the objective was to remove Saddam, disband the military, let the country degrade into chaos never to rise again and reroute hundreds of billions of US tax payers dollars to mostly military related American companies, then again we can say 'mission accomplished'. To claim any other objective would be admitting to miscalculations, political ineptitude and outright military blunders. Somewhere along the way the Administrations objectives changed.

Let's take a fanciful step into the ideal handling of the Iraq campaign. The US ousts the Saddam regime and rolls into Baghdad as it did. It works with the Iraqi generals with which it had communicated prior to the invasion and establishes a bilateral command and control center. After the Iraqi military purges the Saddam loyalists, the US and Iraqi military work together and secure the country in a matter of days. The interm government would be a mix of capable locals and returning exiles whose main duty would be to keep all essential services working. An election committee would guide the country to the elections. And a grateful Iraq would help build permanent US bases and award US companies the government contracts for all oil, military and other services for the next couple of decades. Iraq would be America's strongest ally in the Middle East and Americans would walk hand in hand with Iraqis down peaceful streets. But that's not what happened. Something went terribly askew on the way to the candy store.

Again, this may be sensitive to many that have put trust in one politician over another but we must identify where we are at, how we got here and where we are going. American forces rolled into Iraq after an air assault campaign softened or destroyed vital targets including command and control targets. America took control with relatively little fighting as wars go. The US dismantled the Iraqi army, a move much to the delight of Israel. Israel would much prefer an American occupied Iraq verses an Iraqi army controlled Iraq. The US began the de-baathification process and prevented Baath Party members from any meaningful position or candidacy. Unfortunately, the vast majority of the Baath Party members didn't give a flying frisbee about the Baath Party as it was a required formality for any state job from teachers to technicians. So most of the intelligencia became excluded from the political process.

Likewise, the majority of the military were not particularly loyal to Saddam, some even having plotted to over thrown the regime, but are excluded from the new Iraqi military. Saddam did have that critical mass of loyalists and informants within the military that kept the threat of overthrow to a minimum. Now, with most of the previous Iraqi military's higher officers excluded, the armed forces have to be built up again beginning with privates. In theory, that process could have been scheduled to take up to thirty years or more as the privates are promoted to corporals and then to sergeants until they become generals with America presumably doing the promoting.

The Mukharabaht, or secret police under Saddam, had an informant system that began with little children and went up from there. They did indeed know quite a bit about most anybody that could be a threat or even a potential threat to their way of life. With a network of about 300,000 informants in a country of about 24 million the Iraqi intelligence services did a great job. The US has replaced the Iraqi intelligence services with the CIA. This had severely affected the quality of the information that the US received but did serve to further de-power Iraq. This de-powering of Iraq and keeping it totally dependant for as long as possible seemed to be the US policy.

The US policy towards Iraq seemed to be one of total Iraqi dependency. There is a real danger in this policy for as much as the Iraqis would actually prefer to do business with America as a partner, the climate of excessive American greed and arrogance will drive the Iraqis to other suppliers. And Iran is right next door and very eager to upstage and oust America at every opportunity.

The majority of Iraq's population and parliament are Shiites. Under Saddam the Shiites were persecuted. Many of the prominent Iraqi Shiites in exile that were working towards Saddam's overthrow found support from only one country, Iran. Even during the Iraq/Iran and Gulf Wars when Saddam had Shiite conscripts placed in the front line, Iran welcomed tens of thousands of defectors and loosely maintained them on the chance that they could lead an Iraqi challenge against Saddam. These defectors were headed by a member of the Hakim family, arguably the most powerful family in Iraq today. The Cleric leader of the largest Shiite block in the Iraqi Parliament is also a Hakim. At one time Saddam had 97 members of the Hakim family in prison and with each act of sabotage or resistance by the exiled members of the family Saddam would have some of the imprisoned family executed as punishment. Saddam also had assassins track down other members of the Hakim family in foreign countries as was the case with Said Mehdi Hakim, assassinated in Sudan. For years the Hakim family was relatively safe in Iran. When the first President Bush imposed no-fly zones in Iraq and called upon the Iraqis to rise up, indeed they did. Particularly the Kurds in the Northern mountainous area of Iraq and the Shiites in Southern Iraq. The Shiites began to make gains against Saddam taking control of some cities. Even against armored tanks and artillery the Shiites fought knowing that they could always retreat to the marshes. But when it seemed like Saddam might actually lose control, President Bush lifted the no-fly zone in the South allowing Saddam's helicopter gunships to make short order of the Shiite rebellion, even in the marshes. Again, it was Iran that aided the Shiites, offering refuge and supplies including small arms for the thousands abandoned by the US. There is a long-standing relationship of support between the Shiites in Iraq and Iran that cannot be ignored. This is the reality of the situation today. Even the 'radical' Mukhdah Al Sadr, another Shiite cleric trying to follow in his popular father's path has tremendous support from Iran, albeit in the form of arms and cash used largely for disruptive activities, but support none the less. It is dangerous for the US to under estimate the Iranian connection and loyalties. America's arrogance towards the fledgling political parties did little to win the Iraqi hearts and threatens to drive the Shiites closer to Iran, a prospect not welcomed by most Iraqis.

In Iraq graft, bribery, kickbacks or whatever you want to call it is a way of life. It is expected and practiced as it has been since recorded history. In the US, these practices are frowned upon, discouraged and indeed illegal. In order to circumvent these restrictive regulations the Administration had adopted policies in Iraq of awarding very lucrative contracts with very lenient terms with very little if any oversight. Since the onset of the war, most of the money flowing into Iraq was from the US government. The vast majority of these moneys would go to US companies for projects that were grossly overpriced and were not completed properly if completed at all with few exceptions. The contractors faced little if any competition and certainly not from countries such as Iran. As Iraq's oil revenue grows we can expect to see an increase in the number and amount of contracts awarded to China, Iran and others. In regards to these Iraq based tenders, it is America's greed that handicapped it in competing with China and it's arrogance in competing with Iran. Iran will continue to price its government backed tenders near or even below cost to steal the contracts from America and gain wider access into Iraq. The days of no-bid, fat profit margin contracts with little if any accountability for American companies are gone. Perhaps some companies felt that it was justified and a defendable practice as the rewards must justify the risks. Most of the US contracted services were directly or indirectly in support of the US troops. However, after the initial military action was 'mission accomplished' there was no Al Qaida or sectarian violence in Iraq. Yet Halliburton and subsidiary KBR received multi-billion dollar no-bid contracts on a cost-plus bases. Their cost-plus contracts mean that the more they spend then the more they make. For example, with a 10% margin, a contract for products or services that cost $1 million would be billed at $1.1 million generating $100,000 in profits. But if costs could be inflated to $10 million for the same services then the billing would be for $11 million, generating up to $10 million in profits for delivering the same products or services. This was a powerful motivation to inflate costs and lead some companies to adopt the practice of systematic 'busy work' that put American contract workers and military personnel in harm's way sometimes with deadly consequences. One would think that eventually these company practices that squander tax payer dollars would be brought to justice and restitution be made. Then it is no surprise that Halliburton is moving its headquarters to Qatar, a move that would certainly make prosecution of the company far more difficult. The financial ambitions of the US towards Iraq stood not only to getting those favorable contracts, but to get the Iraqis to sign away their oil for the next thirty years. The US wanted to service the entire Iraqi oil industry from production, transportation, refining, maintenance and sales and be paid in oil. Again, Halliburton would have been in a prime position to service much of such a deal. Towards this end the Bush/Cheney Administration had been hard pressing the

Iraqi government to agree on the distribution of oil proceeds amongst the Kurds, Shiites and Sunnis. This would be the first step needed before a long term deal could be struck. Also included in the 'Iraqi Oil Law' as it was being referred to was provisions to open two thirds of Iraqi oil to foreign interests and the new governing body to include foreign oil companies. Any Iraqi that signed his name to a deal that gave the US exclusive and 'favorable' rights to the country's oil industry for thirty years would have been branded a traitor. He, his family and children would be despised and hated in Iraq yet there are some that would have done it. The US threw its full weight behind a person that had already 'cooperated extensively' with America and tried at every opportunity to support his campaign for power. Ahmed Chalibi, already convicted in Jordan of embezzling double digit millions of dollars from his bank in Jordan, was the US Administration's choice. The US funded his new founded operation with millions of dollars just prior to the Iraq war, in the form or $750,000 per month until he could not properly account for his 'expenses'. The US supported him with additional perks such as the only Iraqi political candidate having photo opportunities with the captured Saddam with publication in the Iraqi press.

But the Iraqis had not had a real election and were scared of the possible outcomes. The Sunnis tried to boycott the elections because they knew that in anything close to a real election that they would lose. This fear was also translated into the Iraqis voting for their primary allegiances, hence the largest political Shiite group (SCIRI headed by one of the Hakim family) won the largest amount of seats and the second largest group, the Kurds voted for the Kurds etc. These political parties are not politics in the US sense of the word but a reflection of primary alliances in a country based upon their strongest divisions such as religious, tribal alliances, Kurdish cultural and sectarianism, much of which the US was remained ignorant until after the fact. At the beginning of the political process, the US tried supporting just the major blocks in Parliament that had effective control. This amounted to the non-Al Sadr based Shiite groups and the Kurds. This simply divided the country into those for and those against American involvement. On a lighter note, it has been said that "If you have two Iraqis you have three political parties". As Americans learned from their mistakes, they eventually moved to supporting all political groups in Parliament except Al Sadr's group thus becoming the common denominator and gaining cooperation from almost all. By adopting a policy of supporting and working with all the political parties, and in particular the tribal leaders, America's biggest advantage is that it curtailed or at least slowed Iranian ambitions in Iraq.

The US and Iran are enemies now and locked in a dance that will lead to war. Ronald Reagan used the Iranians and the hostage crisis as a platform to help get elected. The Iranians cooperated with Reagan and agreed not to return the captives to President Carter. Instead they made them an inauguration gift to Reagan agreeing to turn over a new leaf of sorts. The Iranians kept their end of the bargain but US/Iranian relations continued to deteriorate. Perhaps Reagan genuinely saw them as the enemy or perhaps he just did not want to reverse his campaign stance, but for whatever reason he continued to vilify Iran. This policy continued with President Bush (Sr.) even though there were ample opportunities to improve relations. On several occasions Iran made overtures to the US including preventing 111,000 Pakistani nationals from crossing it's boarders that wanted to join Saddam against the Americans during the first Gulf War. Granted, in this particular instance, any efforts towards Saddam's demise would not be hampered. Iran could have made America's efforts in Afghanistan a fiasco yet it initially chose not to hamper the US campaign in any material way. America's policy of isolating Iran is largely due to Israel's encouragement as well. And as Iran progresses with its nuclear program, the Arab Gulf States, Saudi Arabia in particular will voice increasingly stronger opposition to a nuclear Iran. Israel feels most threatened by Iran's nuclear ambitions. As America increasingly backs Iran into a corner, geo-physically, politically, economically and militarily, Iran will make desperate efforts to win the hearts and souls of the Moslem world. Iran will not use its nuclear power to annihilate Israel, for that would spell the end of Iran and they know it. But Iran would use its nuclear power to force Israel to give the Palestinians a homeland on the West Bank and that would be the greatest Iranian victory possible. America will have to hedge its bet and give the Palestinians a homeland themselves, or at least go through the motions of the same. This will require the US exhorting pressure upon Israel to cooperate until such time as America can increase the military odds of countering an Iranian retaliation in the oil rich Gulf region. Israel may indeed cooperate with the US plan so long as it's assured that Iran's nuclear capability will be eliminated. The only way that any US administration can guarantee such a result will be to guarantee to attack the Iranian nuclear industry before Iran reaches full nuclear arms production capability. Dealing a crushing blow to the Iranian nuclear program could be done at arm's length with less than 200 cruise missiles and a few score of the deep penetrating bombs that the US now has. But to leave the Iranian military untouched after such an action would invite certain devastation to much if not all of the oil producing capacity of the entire Gulf region. The Iranian Air force and long range missile capacity would also have to be targeted. Iran's navy would also pose a threat to oil terminals and production platforms as would smaller sea going craft that could be outfitted with short range missiles. It would almost be easier for America to knock out Iran's total infrastructure and just hold out for the week or two that it would take Iran to descend into total chaos, but that's not the way the world works, for now. The US has the capability to deliver very measured actions and will exercise the same. The big questions are 'How measured an action?' and 'When?'

The US has Iran almost totally surrounded by land and sea. It has over 200,000 troops and two to four carrier groups in the immediate vicinity of Iran at any given time. Yet it needs time, not to avert the inevitable Iranian confrontation, rather to better prepare, and that includes Israel. The US needs time to deploy the latest anti-missile weaponry throughout the region and in particular in Israel and the Gulf. It also needs time to deploy the most sophisticated electronic airborne jamming equipment so that when the strike upon Iran commences, then all Iranian communications shut down. This shut down is not just the traditional radar jamming to protect the aircraft stuff but the latest virtually total shutdown of all communications including cell phones, radio and television. In short, the first wave of aircraft or drones will totally neutralize any and all transmissions over the airwaves. From there, the target pickings are easy, with little if any counter moves against such actions. Again, the launch of these strikes will certainly be before Iran can enjoy any measurable nuclear arms production. In regards to the targets, a 'guestimate' would be most if not all of the nearly 300 fixed sites directly associated with Iran's nuclear program, Iran' air force, navy and any mobile and fixed missile launch vehicles that can be readily targeted. That would be the minimum 'guestimate' for a prudent military action. Any less and the US would be jeopardizing the Gulf oil by leaving an angry and capable adversary. Anymore and it would greatly increase civilian casualties and be considered an attack on the country instead of a regime policy. The only US ground troop applications on Iranian territory would be the possible securing certain sites such as oil terminals and production platforms and the occupation of certain Iranian islands and coastal areas that could threaten shipping in the region. It is conceivable that Iran could literally dump 3 million barrels of their own oil or more per day directly into the Gulf. The currant in the Gulf circulates northwest along the Iranian coast up to Iraq and Kuwait, then back down along the Saudi coast and Emirates. In one month Iran could dump ten billion gallons of crude in the 90,000 sq. mile Gulf rendering sizable 'no-go areas'. Add to that the float or oil in storage waiting to be exported and if Iran were to be successful in damaging the Arab oil facilities in the Gulf then that figure could increase eight fold or more.

The dilemma for the US President will be whether to enact the most minimal strike of about forty to forty five nuclear related targets that would set back the Iranian program years and risk inviting retaliation from an intact Iranian military, or strike the approximately 300 nuclear related sites coupled with a crippling blow to the military with perhaps a dose of destabilizing assault on the fragile Iranian infrastructure or something in between. To narrow the range, the President will probably fall short of an all out strike and most probably chose to target 150 to 200 Iranian nuclear sites, plus the front line retaliation capability of the Iranians. Such an action would be described as necessary to stop Iran's nuclear program and greatly diminish Iran's retaliatory capability. And such an attack would be far short of the damage of which the US is capable. Iran knows that if it attacks Israel directly that it will lose. Iran also knows that taking on the US military directly is futile. It will retaliate in a different way. These events will probably transpire before the end of 2012.

There is no official deadline for a US strike against Iran, however, several other parties can force an ultimatum. Israel could privately or publically threaten attack. Israel does not want weapons inspectors in Iran, it wants Iran's nuclear and conventional weapons capability smashed and preferably the Ayatollahs gone. Israel will continue to urge the US President to strike Iran before they achieve nuclear weapons capability. Israel cannot risk the US president negotiating and negotiating with Iran until Iran has 'the bomb'. At that point the rules change and Iran can easily win the hearts of the 150 million Arabs in the Middle East as it forces Israel to the table to give the Palestinians a homeland. Israel will exert all its considerable influence on the US President to attack Iran at the earliest instance. Every day that passes is another day closer for Iran gaining nuclear capability and they are working 24-7 towards that end. If the US shows signs of an imminent strike too early then Iran may strike first. Sooner or later the US always does Israel's bidding. Preparations for the final battle are already being made by all sides.

IRAQ

In 1968 a Baathist coup lead by five generals and one colonel, overthrew the Iraqi President and took control of the country. That colonel was Saddam Hussein. In the years that followed he continued to gain power. He even killed his superior and when nobody wanted to fill the position, he filled it himself. By 1979 he was effectively running the country. Soon afterwards he became President and Prime Minister and began his reign of terror in earnest.

Next door, in Iran, the Islamic revolution had ousted the pro-US Shah and was taking hold. With Reagan becoming president, the US embassy hostages in Tehran and the weakened Iranian military from the 'purges', Saddam had a green light to go after the oil rich area of the Shatt-al-Arab waterway. Saddam began to receive support from the US and the Gulf States that feared the spread of the Iranian Islamic style revolution. The support from the Gulf countries came mostly in financial form. Saddam was indeed battling the Iranians, something the Gulf states approved of, but they were also scared of him and certainly did not want to offend him. The US also supplied financial aid, albeit in a very roundabout way and added the military support. The US used the Ex-Im Bank (Export Import Bank used to advance and guarantee payment on large overseas trade transactions) to guarantee approximately three billion dollars worth of US grain sales to Iraq. Large amounts of the grain was re-routed to Eastern European countries in exchange for weapons and munitions destined for Iraq. Much of the US support for Iraq was orchestrated by the CIA and conducted through a network of some 160 companies both domestic and foreign, including the infamous Banc de Lavro. The exacts of the transactions are still shrouded under the CIA veil of secrecy.

Saddam used the war to eliminate many of the young rebellious Shiite men that filled his prisons by offering them amnesty in exchange for military service. These were used in the front line against Iran. Saddam also purged Iraq of anybody that could be of any threat to him. Nobody was beyond Saddam's wrath from successful generals that were achieving hero status to his son-in-laws to the common man on the street. During Saddam's reign, several hundred thousand Iraqis were tortured, killed, or otherwise disappeared. The result of this policy was to create a real political vacuum. The country was in a tight grip of fear and paranoia.

Saddam's Mukharabaht (Secret Police) and their network of informants numbered close to 300,000 in a country with a population of 20 million. Saddam's personal security was second to none in the world costing an estimated $2-$3 billion per year. His fear of assassination prompted him to have multiple 'doubles' that would motorcade to and from his palaces and other sites. He also would never spend more than six hours at any location, or sleep in the same place twice in a row. At the height of the pressure against Saddam, even his personal body guard contingent was not trusted and where he had say 20 armed guards, maybe three would have live ammunition and no one knew who did or didn't have the live rounds. Many people that have shook Saddam's hand had to have theirs dipped in a solution that would neutralize poisons prior to the shaking. Saddam was fond of poisons as he used some to kill his adversaries or some that would not be kill immediately but cast into extremely painful state of being for the rest of their life. He used various chemicals on the Kurds wiping out 5,000 in Sulymania, and used vast amounts of chemicals on the Iranians once they managed a counter offensive and crossed over into Iraqi territory. Thousands of Iranians killed and many more thousands injured from the effects of chemical warfare. Artillery shells delivered the chemical agents. Saddam also had SCUDs capable of delivering chemical or conventional warheads. He had initiated work on a nuclear power plant that the Israelis destroyed. And even a 'super gun', a giant fixed cannon capable of firing a projectile into low orbit, also thought to be scuttled by the Israelis. These policies made Saddam a feared man both in country and in the Middle East neighborhood East of the Mediterranean. The prevailing sentiment from the leaders of the Arab neighbors of Saddam could be summed up as 'they wished him well but wished him far away'. Saddam's ruthless grip on the country effectively reduced the meaningful population of Iraq to one, himself. There was no 'national budget' but rather a system that all revenues from the oil industry and the many other businesses that he confiscated went straight into his pocket and all payments made, such as 'social security' would be made known to have come from Saddam personally. This made it very easy for the US to deal with Iraq in that there were no challenges to his word whatsoever. It was also like having a tiger by the tail in that the US was fixed to him. Saddam demonstrated his disapproval of the US dealing with Iran over the 'Iran-Contra' fiasco just a day and a half after the US/Iran relationship became public by attacking the USS Cole with Exocit missiles, killing over three dozen US Sailors. Though Saddam 'settled' with the families of the sailors privately for a sum rumored to be one million dollars each, he was sending a clear message to the US and that was pick sides between himself and Iran. The US choose Saddam and less than two months later the US stepped up the 'thwarting' of Iran in earnest with attacks on Iranian oil facilities in the Gulf and culminating in the downing of a routine Iranian civilian airliner flight over the Gulf resulting in over two hundred civilian men, women and children dead. The US had provided Saddam with real-time satellite intelligence of Iranian troop positions and movement enabling the Iraqi Army to counter the Iranian maneuvers with high casualty figures for the Iranians. It seemed that the sides were chosen.

Saddam concluded that the US did indeed support him, not realizing that it was simply a case of 'the enemy of my enemy is my friend' and Iran was America's enemy. The Iraq/Iran War lasted eight years. The hostilities ended with no change of boarders. Saddam's expansionist ambitions were thwarted to the East. To the North of Iraq lies Turkey, a powerful country of seventy million people and an ally of America. To the West was Jordan and Syria, both poor countries and dangerously close to Israel. To the South was oil rich Kuwait. When Saddam saw that Kuwait was treating all the money it had given to Saddam for the Iraq/Iran war as debt instead of a gift or aid, then Saddam had his reason for invading. Besides Kuwait was part of 'Iraq' until the English carved it out. Three weeks before the Saddam's invasion of Kuwait, he had a column of tanks and troop transports on the boarder stretching over 37 miles (60 kilometers) on the main highway connecting the two countries. Saddam also had advance reconnaissance teams that had taken up positions on the two Kuwaiti islands off the coast. Saddam was waiting for the US reaction as his intention was clear. The US ambassador to Iraq conveyed the US stance as it was not the policy of the US to get involved in boarder disputes. This seems to suggest that

America was encouraging Saddam to invade, as Kuwait is barely 100 miles from its Northern border with Iraq to its Southern border with Saudi Arabia.

Saddam invaded Kuwait and immediately increased his oil production from 3 mbd (million barrels per day) to 4.5 mbd. He quietly offered the US cheaper oil but the US quietly declined as they prepared to take down Saddam's military a few notches. The Kuwaiti Royal family evacuated to Saudi Arabia and took up residence in the Saudi King's summer palace in mountain city of Taif. Saddam pillaged Kuwait as the US rallied much of the world against the invasion. Under a United Nations mandate the US lead forces commenced Desert Storm. The US conducted an aerial campaign lasting seven weeks. The Iraqi Air force was the first casualty as they were no match for the far superior American aircraft. Some of the Iraqi pilots flew their jets to Iran. The first few of these aircraft were shot at, but when the Iranians realized that they were trying to land they welcomed this 'manna from heaven'. During this phase of the campaign over 100,000 sorties were flown causing the destruction of primary, secondary and even tertiary targets. After seven weeks the infrastructure of Iraq was totally crippled and the Iraqi military demoralized. Many high ranking Iraqi officers watched helplessly as their country was destroyed and began turning against Saddam. Some had communicated with the US expressing their desire to overthrow Saddam but the US had other plans. The opening action of the ground war began with a small column of Iraqi tanks and troops apparently wanting to defect near the Kuwait/Saudi coastal border. With tank turrets turned backwards the Iraqi's crossed into Saudi Arabia then, instead of surrendering, they engaged the coalition. This was to discourage any further defections from the Iraqi forces, as the coalition became dubious of any surrender attempts. The ground war lasted 100 hours and reduced Iraq's military even further. The defections were in the tens of thousands with Iraqi soldiers sometime crossing minefields in order to surrender. As the Iraqi forces withdrew from Kuwait City they were annihilated. General Shwartzkoff's tactics had cut off the Iraqi retreat. As the General prepared to annihilate the Republican Guard, the best and last forces of the Iraqi Army still loyal to Saddam, President Bush (Sr.) ordered a cease-fire. Eliminating the Republican Guard would all but guarantee Saddam's demise and that was not what the US had in mind. In all probability, General Shwartzkoff could have accomplished a crushing defeat of the Republican Guard within 50 hours leaving Saddam defenseless from his own regular army. Instead, the US imposed large no-fly zones in both the North and South of the country. War reparations were demanded and UN sanctions put in place as weapons inspector began searching the country for chemical and biological weapons and the 32 SCUD missiles that were unaccounted for. President Bush called upon the Iraqi people to rise up and overthrow Saddam and indeed they began. The Kurds had made great gains in securing much of their mountainous terrain. This was possible because of the lack of Iraqi air support. In the South, the Shiites began their uprising and succeeded in taking several cities, driving out the Iraqi forces. Saddam was losing the war in the oil rich Southern third of the country until the US eased the no-fly restrictions and allowed the Iraqi helicopter gunships to quell the Shiite rebellion in the South. The Shiites took to the marshes to evade the tanks and artillery, but were still being hunted down by helicopters. Some of these

Shiites made it to Iran, but most did not. Both Desert Storm and the rebellion ended and Saddam remained in power.

With Saddam in power, Iran could not expand its movement Westward, the entire Gulf region would have to re-militarize and the US, via UN sanctions, could control three million barrels of oil per day of Iraqi oil. Perhaps the greatest US casualties of Desert Storm were General Shwartzkoff and General Colin Powel. Two lifelong military geniuses that delivered the greatest military victory in US history, with a casualty ratio of 1,000:1, both resigned soon afterwards. In the years following the 'cease-fire' of Desert Storm, Saudi Arabia, Kuwait and the rest of the Gulf States bought several hundred billion dollars worth of primarily US military hardware, systems and support. The US also gained military bases in the region. Even though the weapon inspectors found and destroyed thousands of artillery chemical warheads, Saddam still made a mockery of their efforts. Saddam was still in power and began smuggling out oil to sell on the black market. The US allowed this practice along with other violations of the sanctions. In Southern Iraq, where stockpiles of chemical weapons had been destroyed and large use of radioactive DU (depleted uranium) rounds were used, birth defects and cancer rates began to climb to tenfold the normal rates. Throughout most of the country where potable water and medicines were in short supply deaths from common diseases began to soar. The sanctions were taking a toll on the common people. Much of the medicines that were destined for the populace were collected by Saddam's regime and sold on the black market. Increased pressure upon the civilian population meant increased security pressures for Saddam. Two of his son-in-laws defected to Jordan and were debriefed by the US as they had held positions in the regime that entitled them to some of the most sensitive information on WMDs. Saddam forgave them, granted them amnesty and upon their return had them killed. Whatever information they may have disclosed about Saddam's secret military operations were quickly mooted by Saddam as he was a master of deception and hiding things, including himself. For years Saddam had built large, secret underground bunkers, the true number and location never having been confirmed. Saddam began looking for a new cause to aid in his propaganda war. The Palestinians were always a convenient cause as used by the Syrians, Iranians and others when it suited them. Saddam began supporting the Palestinians by donating $25,000 to the families of suicide bombers. This was a charitable act designed to gain sympathy and support of the Arab World to play against the long standing Israeli policy to bulldoze the house of a suicide bomber's family, leaving them destitute on the streets. But Saddam's support of the suicide bombers' families became one more excuse for President G.W. Bush to launch his search for WMD's and the overthrow of the regime. This time the US ambitions were different, the overthrow of Saddam and obtaining the oil business of Iraq in whatever form and by whatever means.

As the American troops poured into Baghdad, the resistance seemed to fade away. Sporadic 'hit and run' tactics replaced regular military engagements. The Americans were treated as saviors and rightly so as they had released the country from the death grip of a most brutal dictator. The Iraqi Army was disbanded as was the intelligence agencies and many of the food and medicine distribution networks. De-Baathification was the order of the day. Anyone who was a member of the Baathist Party was prohibited from any meaningful government related job. As the old bureaucracy crumbled here was an almost total disruption of most government services and jobs. Unemployment skyrocketed and everything was subject to being stolen. As Chicago was once famed for its gangsters, Baghdad was famed for its thieves and they began to go to work. As the Iraqi army was decommissioned, most of Saddam's huge military stockpiles were looted. Priceless museum artifacts of the beginnings of civilization disappeared. Abandoned factories were striped and electrical pylons were downed, dismantled and resold for scrap. Even the destroyed military vehicles that had been hit with radioactive DU rounds were dismantled by hand for recycling. Life in Iraq was degrading to hand-to-mouth subsistence. Inflation became rampant as Iraqi dinars continued to flood the market. Saddam used to have one of the currency printing presses in one of his palaces, but others may have been used by Saddam or his loyalists during the early occupation. The US decided to change the currency and printed new money to be exchanged for the old. There was a huge shortfall in the estimated amount of new currency required necessitating an almost tripling of the initial number of bills. Much of this 'new currency' went into the hands of Saddam loyalists as they were the ones with the majority of the old currency. Inadvertently, the US was funding the loyalists with the new stabilized currency. Many of Saddam's regime escaped with family in tow to Syria and Yemen. Others stayed to carry on the fight. America has made many enemies in recent years and all saw Iraq as a chance to strike a blow at her. Saudi extremists, Syrians, Al Qaida, Saddam loyalists, Iraqi Sunnis, Iranians, Shiites extremists, the list goes on. Some groups had the 'hometown advantage', some came with training, weapons and finance, all came with dedication and the ambition of defeating America or at the very least to give her a stinging black eye to remember.

The US handling of Iraq seemed more concerned with de-powering the country and maintaining its dependency upon the US than to institute order. The boarders became more and more porous allowing that critical mass of support against America to enter. The US busied itself with recycling billions of dollars of 'redevelopment' and service contracts through the country with little if any accountability. The US soldiers, trained to take on and defeat any military in the world were increasingly faced with a new enemy. Guerilla Warfare in an urban environment where the locals are supposed to be 'friendlies' was unfamiliar to the common soldier manning a checkpoint. Suicide bombers were a totally different adversary than the boot camp trained US soldiers. As a consequence, some of the ill-prepared US soldiers began adopting a more trigger happy philosophy of 'shoot first and ask questions later'. When you are in a crowded urban setting and come under fire and you do not know from where the fire is originating, then what do you do? You fire back. But where? Everywhere. At whom do you fire? Everyone in the immediate area. What do you do when a car approaches your checkpoint at an uncomfortable speed, i.e. too fast for you to assess the potential danger? You fire at it, even if it is a warning shot or one meant to disable the vehicle. This unofficial policy may have reduced the immediate threat to a number of US soldiers, but it also gave rise to a division with the Iraqi nationals. Such random acts were high-octane fuel in the propaganda war against America. The American enemies began to organize, strategize and adapt against 'the occupation'. Roadside bombs against US troop movements and the giving of high priority to targeting any locals that assisted the Americans in any way forced a deeper separation with the locals, particularly in the larger urban areas where proximity of the locals and Americans was a fact of life. There was an increasing amount of danger for anyone in close proximity to American soldiers as IED's (Improvised Explosive Devices) were quite indiscriminant when they exploded. Yet there remained strong support for the Americans with some of the population. Events such as the Abu Ghrab Prison abuse did little for the US cause.

The Kurds in the North were beginning to prosper after years of relative hardship and were almost autonomous. As the first Iraqi elections drew closer the two main rival Kurdish organizations settled their differences and joined to present a unified political front. For years the Kurds have been somewhat under the protection of the US but are still a complex problem. They have their own language and culture and want independence. They have been used and abused by Iraq, Turkey and Iran throughout recent history and want their own homeland. The approximately 5 million Kurds in Northern Iraq have come closest to independence yet there are millions more in the neighboring areas of Turkey and Iran. If the Kurds ever gained independence in Iraq then about ten minutes later the Turks would invade and take control.

The US began to deal with the 'Tribal Leaders' in Iraq. This had been a long neglected element of the US efforts as there is nothing really comparable in the US society. By neglecting the Iraqi tribal hierarchy, the US was in fact insulting them. The tribal loyalties have served the Iraqis since recorded history and is not easily discarded. It is relatively easy to gain their cooperation in most cases by the use of simple protocol, diplomacy and dollars. If one wants to do something on 'their turf' or involving 'their clan', then one approaches the tribal leader first, through channels if necessary. Diplomatically paying ones respects and presenting the case that requires his help. So long as one has 'paid' their respects properly and allow him to be magnanimous in front of his clan then he would be a fool to refuse anyone knowing that the wrath of hell can be called down from above upon him. By using protocol and humble diplomacy the US gained many tribal leaders' support. This policy directly translated into an on the ground network of informants and enforcers that create relatively trouble free zones. It was the critical mass of 'grass roots' support that was so desperately needed to stabilize the streets. The Iraqis are highly ranked in the 'busy-body index' and are nosy about their neighbors to no end. At one end of the spectrum the Iraqi 'rumor mill' is always in warp drive. At the other end of the spectrum, their 'neighborhood watch' program is second to none. Neighborhood locals 'know' when an outsider doesn't fit in. The 'Chikhanas' (tea cafes) have always been full of dialogues and gossip concerning some stranger's name, family, wealth, history and postulations regarding true intentions.

A progression of this policy would be that the US empowers not just the tribal leaders, Sheiks, Religious leaders and other assorted powerhouses, but also empowers the police and army with the tools and training that they need. The US would soon be looking eye to eye with a strong, rich, powerful and loyal ally in the Middle East. Unfortunately, that wasn't in the 'Forward Looking Statement' of the Halliburton annual report. These lessons were only being learned the hard way by the US military and implemented out of pure necessity to reduce US casualties instead of being a pre-war policy of the State Department and Administration.

The US is caught in Iraq between the ideal relationship and the worst case scenario and tending towards the latter. It is a fluid relationship with mistakes being made by both sides right from the start. Whatever financial, military, political, propaganda and personal intentions the US had before they engaged in the occupation of Iraq, they were not founded in reality for the long term, as time has borne out. The US has used Iraq through which to 'recycle' hundreds of billions of dollars of inflated contracts with little if any accountability to the US taxpayers that will ultimately pay the bill. The US has gained long term military bases, out in the middle of nowhere, distanced and buffered from anything threatening or meaningful. And that's about it. Except that there might be an element of personal satisfaction by President Bush (W.) effecting the execution of Saddam who had made an attempt upon President Bush senoir. On the Iraqi side, they have learned that in their eagerness to dispose of Saddam they have jumped out of the frying pan. Where they land is still to be determined and they are quickly learning that through Iraqi unity that they can extend that diplomatic 'hang time' before choosing a landing. The first Iraqi elections were to a public that was largely ignorant of any real electoral process. Political parties sprang up from seemingly nowhere vying for a chance at representation. It seemed that if you had two Iraqi politicians, then you had three political parties. Ignorance and even outright fear gripped the population as they voted for their closest 'political' associations. Hence, the Shiite group formerly known as SCIRI, won the largest single block in Parliament. This is the backbone of the Iraqi government and the group is lead by Abdul Azziz Al Hakim. It had the blessings of Sistanni, the highest Iraqi Shiite Cleric, enough said. The Kurds, fearing being lost in the possible myriad of potential candidates, unified and came across with the second largest single block. Sunni, secular and other groups constituted the rest. These representatives in the new Iraqi government were elected for the most part because of loyalties and not based upon political adeptness, capability and the greatly needed inter-mediation. The problem is that many, if not most, of the representation would not be there if not for Iran. Certainly, Al Hakim, one of the relative moderates of the Shiite blocks, owes his existence largely for the support and refuge he received from Iran during the time that US supported Saddam who was trying to assassinate him. There are others that owe varying degrees of loyalty to Iran as well, particularly within the Shiite community. Most of the Shiite power has come from the demise of Saddam and the Sunnis that ruled Iraq for the past few decades. The Sunnis have lost their power base and control of the vast majority of government jobs doled out to 'friends and family'. Industry has begun from scratch and there is little room for the Sunnis particularly while sectarian violence divides the country. The Shiite Sunni rivalry may lessen from militia actions to just animosity but the divide is there. The Sunnis still have a substantial amount of wealth but gone is their grip on the country. As for the Kurds, they have their own culture and language. By definition, an 'Arab' is one whose mother tongue is Arabic. The Kurdish language is not Arabic in the true sense and probably closer to Farsi. The Kurdish culture evolved in the mountainous regions of Northern Iraq, Western Iran and South East Turkey, yet they have become an integral part of Iraq. Since 1991 the Kurds have enjoyed a taste of autonomy under the protection of the US. Once tasted, freedom is always coveted and will be defended. The Kurds will continue to be the 'swing vote' in the Iraqi Parliament and adds a level of complexity to the political scene.

The Kurds in Turkey and Iran would love to enjoy similar circumstances as their Iraqi neighbors and even form a nation. It will not happen, but the desire is there. It presents dilemmas with Turkey as the armed Kurds from Iraq continue to attack Turkish authorities in the region. The Iraqi Kurds and the Turks both have strong relationships with the US. Iraqi 'Kurdistan' is also a backdoor to Iran in the mountainous and rugged North East of Iraq, a convenient door for the US if the US can maintain its dominant position there.

The other Iraqi minorities are only important as leveraged support by the larger political parties. They have no real political or economic base that would give them any substantial power in Parliament and have to side with the larger interests to secure their positions.

The US has built and continues to build its military bases in Iraq for its long term presence. This acts to insure that Iraq does not fall into the hands of unfriendly forces and to halt any Iranian ground expansion westward. But the most important issue regarding Iraq is oil. The proven reserves of Iraq are 114 billion barrels. At $90 per barrel that equates to $10 trillion. This is Iraq's wealth and the underlying reason for much of the past US policies regarding the country. Much of the Iraqi oil is 'light' meaning it is much easier and cheaper to refine and has a more favorable ratio of the higher end distillates such as gasoline and kerosene than heavier crude. Iraqi oil is easy and cheap to reach unlike most of today's offshore or deep drilling for new production. The US has a little more than half a million wells producing almost five and a half million barrels of oil per day. That averages about 10 barrels of oil per day per well. Iraqi oil production peaked pre-war at 3.5 million barrels per day from about 1,700 wells or an average of over 2,000 barrels of oil per day per well. These factors alone make the Iraqi oil industry very attractive. But the Iraqi oil industry is in dire need of a near complete overhaul. Over the years it has fallen into disarray with a corresponding drop in production down to around two million barrels per day. Iraq needs refurbishing their existing oil industry in nearly every facet of operations. That includes production with existing and new wells, the distribution network with existing and new pipelines and pumping stations and refining as Iraq now has to import much of its gasoline and kerosene requirements. Tens of billions of dollars worth of work needs to be done for Iraq to reach anywhere near its oil producing capability The security issue, if resolved, means that the profit margins can be increased as proven out by currant contractors in Iraq operating under threatening conditions.

The proven reserves are from decades old data and do not reflect the vast amount of natural gas, also undeveloped in country. The 'suspected' reserves of oil would at least double and possibly triple the existing figures, again, without even developing the natural gas. To put this amount in perspective, Iraq could supply all the US with all its imported oil needs for the next fifty years. Most of the oil in the region and certainly all of the 'mega-fields' are in a band that runs the length of the Gulf, up through Iraq and up in to the Caspian Sea. Iraq is right in the middle of this band with large oil fields in the North and larger ones in the South. It is strongly suspected that there are huge deposits in the Western Desert area and possibly in the central region. Iraq could be the next 'Saudi Arabia' if given the chance. The developing of this 'new oil' will be a windfall for the companies involved for decades to come. The interest is high from the US oil companies even though little new geological data has been gathered officially. Perhaps their interest is peaked by reviewing the old data but employing new analysis techniques. Regardless of the data available publicly, refurbishing, developing and maintaining the Iraqi oil industry would conveniently explain why the US had been most hesitant to return any meaningful power back to the Iraqis until they got signed contracts for long term commitments for this oil business. This 'high-handed' pressure by the US has been employed for years with no results. Perhaps the only result is that it has forced the withdrawal of most of the American troops. The American troops that remain will increasingly become targets for Iranian backed 'militias' and terrorist cells. But the oil business is unique and this is not something that the US oil companies or the administration is likely to leave up to chance, not with hundreds of billions of dollars worth of new, highly profitable business at stake let alone the security of the entire region. So, Iraq's fate is tied to the US Administration's policy, which is tied economically and militarily to the oil industry and Israel, respectively and all set to 'finalize' before the Iranians obtain nuclear weapons production capability.

SAUDI ARABIA

Saudi Arabia is a phenomenal kingdom lead by about fifty individuals with little if any accountability to anyone outside their clique. They quietly exercise power that they have gleamed from three sources. First and foremost they are the keepers of Islam with the Islamic sites of Mecca and Medina. These are more than just Holy Shrines as it is one of the five pillars of Islam to make the pilgrimage to Mecca at least once in every Moslem's life. Over a billion Moslems worldwide should, in theory, make the Hajj or pilgrimage. Secondly, Saudi Arabia exports around ten million barrels of oil a day to an oil thirsty world and is the backbone of OPEC. Thirdly, Saudi Arabia has close ties with the US. These three factors has enabled the Kingdom to leverage their power into phenomenal wealth and political power. This immense wealth and power is vested in the hands of a few dozen individuals that have very different priorities and concerns than the average voting American. The concerns of this 'Clique' that runs the country are self preservation, self promotion and 'other' causes in that order. There is the Royalty, but only about 10% of the 2000 princes and princesses have great wealth and power. There are the technocrats and the super-merchants. These three groups effectively rule and run the country's wealth. Matters are complicated by the fact that this 'Gentry', are immensely wealthy and powerful. Take, for example the Bin Laden family. The grandfather of the existing Bin Laden generation was a building contractor that won the contract to rebuild Mecca, the Holiest of Holy sites of Islam. Since then the Bin Laden family has had an effective 'first option' on many major construction contracts tendered in country. The family is now worth in the region of thirty billion dollars plus. Osama, the brother of the head of the Bin Laden family was the activist and felt the cause to fight the Russians when they occupied Afghanistan, a Moslem country. While fighting the Russians, Osama received training, weapons and other assistance from the CIA. When the Russians left Afghanistan the support from the CIA to Osama stopped. He felt abandoned afterwards and held a grudge, particularly when his offer to the Saudi elite to oust Saddam from Kuwait with his forces was refuted and instead was replace with the Saudis allowing the 'infidel' US troops to hold camp in Saudi Arabia. There are thousands, perhaps tens of thousands of individuals that have been used by the US and then abandoned but not many with a personal wealth in the region of two hundred million dollars. It is one thing to offend or double-cross an impoverished rebel where he might throw a Molotov cocktail at a target of opportunity. It is another matter to offend the wealthy organizer and leader of a rebel force that you have trained in dirty guerilla tactics. It is conceivable that no one is willing to track down Osama for the twenty five million dollar bounty for fear that Osama's brother may place a much larger bounty for revenge. Placing a bounty on a family member of a prominent Saudi family seems to be for show.

Many Saudis support various radical elements mostly taking place out of country. Various Palestinian elements, Al Qaida and insurgents in Iraq and in the region all receive funding some of which is suspected as originating from wealthy Saudi individuals.

The Saudis are a double edged sword in that they can, by the stroke of a pen, raise the price of crude oil to well over two hundred or three hundred dollars a barrel. By the same token they can and have prevented others from attempting the same. In years past, before world demand for crude pressed production limits, Saudi Arabia carried the only stick that could break the back of OPEC, not that it wanted to. Before the first Gulf war Saudi Arabia was producing four million barrels a day and the only OPEC member with a production capacity of eleven million barrels a day. They could have flooded the market with oil. Their suggestions or demands within OPEC were usually heeded. Now, they produce ten million barrels a day with a spare capacity of about a million additional barrels but of very heavy, high sulfur crude. They are the only Arab oil exporter with that kind of spare capacity. Iraq is a long term threat to Saudi Arabia's standing in OPEC and the world oil community. It is not in Saudi Arabia's interest to have Iraq join their league of being able to produce ten million barrels a day.

America and Saudi Arabia have enjoyed a close relationship for decades. There are some that do not approve of this relationship, personified by Osama Bin Laden, who feel that the US helps maintain a corrupt regime interested in lining their own pockets at the expense of national interests. But the 'traditional' skim off of contracts and other expenditures is normally around just 5%, far too little to adversely affect the budget of a wealthy country such as Saudi Arabia. 5% is common place throughout the Middle East and is not out of line for someone in a power position, it is even expected. Saudi Arabia and the other wealthy countries in the Middle East have been generous to their friends, family and others. They understand the 'trickle down' theory, perhaps even invented it. This skim, bribe or whatever you want to call it is a way of life and extends across most of their GNP. The Saudi ruling clique is, without doubt, the richest collection of individuals in the world and without having made the 'Fortune 500' list. They have used their fortunes to leverage up their power by investing not just in businesses but in people. Whether it's a colonel that becomes president of a Middle East country or a failing Texas oilman the Saudi's know how to make friends and influence people using their money.

At ten million barrels of oil a day in a world that consumes 70 to 80 million barrels a day gives the Saudi's immense power. They could single handedly or collectively spearhead the threat of an oil embargo against the world unless Israel reaches peace and parody with a new Palestinian state. They could certainly fund a war with the best weapons and training money can buy. This is what some radical elements in the Middle East would like to see happen. But there is no profit in it, only downside financial risk. Instead, the Saudi's have embarked upon a massive campaign to maintain and secure the flow of oil to the world in the event of the Iranians disrupting the tanker traffic through the Strait of Hormuz, the bottle neck that connects the Gulf to the Indian Ocean and beyond. They are joined by others in the region to reroute pipelines around the Strait of Hormuz and even cross country to the Red Sea or Mediterranean. They have recently established a dedicated force starting with 5,000 to exclusively protect the oil installations and infrastructure. This number is set to quickly grow to 35,000 troops, equipped with the latest technology. This is a multi-billion dollar program and attests to the seriousness with which they regard the Iranian threat. It seems that they feel that an Iranian action of sorts is a very high probability at the very least.

For all of Saudi Arabia's wealth and power, it is still just a fragile monarchy run by just fifty or so individuals. It is also a prize that Iran dearly covets. Iran with influence, let alone control over Saudi Arabia's oil would speed them upon their objective of converting the world to their kind of Islam. It will not happen.

TURKEY

Turkey is instrumental in the coming Jihad. It has a population of about 75 million and is the bridge between Iran and Europe. It is not Arab and tolerated at best by most in the Arab World. It has steadily been moving in a more Islamic direction through its parliament. The Turkish military is something all together different, literally. It is kept separate from the population and indeed the government and has 'overturned' four election results when it deemed that the election of a religious majority was not in Turkey's best interest. The military has long since held in check any radical Islamic efforts to seize control of the government but that stance may be moderating as representation of the Islamic majority continues to grow. It has and has had strong relations with the US. First during the cold war with at least nine radar stations to monitor Soviet air movements. Use of airbases have also been of great value to the US as a threat to the Soviet Union and as a gateway to Iraq. During the first Gulf War, Turkish airspace and airbases were used extensively. And again during the takeover of Iraq. The Turkish military have supported for the most part US policy in the Middle East for decades cooperating with support concerning the Soviet Union, Israel, Iraq and more. It has the second largest military within NATO, second only to America.

Turkey has been trying to gain admission to the EU since it was the EEC but to no avail. Turkey, with its somewhat barbaric stance on human rights would be an open backdoor to Europe for every undesirable in the Middle East and that will just not be tolerated. Any public efforts to the contrary are for diplomatic 'stall time' to slow Turkeys shift from Western to Middle Eastern political and religious alignment.

Turkey is far more than just a land bridge to Europe. It is the make or break of any Jihad that originates in Iran. If Turkey is against a Jihad that originates in Iran, then it pretty much stops there. Iran and Turkey are of similar populations of about 75 million giving each the capacity to raise a formidable fighting force of several million, if hard pressed. Much of the terrain in Turkey is rugged and easily defendable from an invading force. In a dual between the two countries, both would expend much of their fighting capacity just neutralizing the other. Iran would have to deal with Turkey directly or indirectly. Iran could not afford to expand in any other direction and leave it's boarder with Turkey unprotected. An Iran with the bulk of its military force engaged elsewhere would be an open invitation to a hostile Turkey. A direct confrontation with Turkey would leave so few troops remaining at the end of the conflict that they would be little threat to anyone.

The reverse has even greater implications. An Iranian/Turkish alliance would create a formidable foe that would be very difficult to contain or combat. Such an alliance would span from Pakistan and Afghanistan, along the Indian Ocean to the Strait of Hormuz, along the entire Eastern coast of the Gulf, the entire Eastern and Northern boarder of Iraq, into the Mediterranean, Caspian and Black Seas with full control of Istanbul and land borders with Europe. All the oil from Northern Iraq, up to one million barrels per day, is piped into Turkey then out through Turkey to the Mediterranean. Shipping between the Black Sea ports and the

Mediterranean would be controlled by the Turks and passage through the Strait of Hormuz would be in grave danger of coming to a complete halt. Much of the Caspian Sea oil would be perilously close to Iran. Much of the transport of the rest would be perilously close to Turkey or bottlenecked in the Black Sea. An Iranian/Turkish Alliance would mean that the Gulf, Caspian, Black Sea, Aegean Sea and the Eastern Mediterranean would be threatened at the very least, probably neutralized and possibly dominated.

Tactically, an Iranian instigated Jihad without Turkey subscribing to the cause could mean disruption to the Gulf oil supplies, further and possibly total chaos in Iraq and threats to Caspian oil production. Missile threats from Iran would be limited to largely Middle Eastern targets. There would not be a land-based invasion in to Europe or campaign to take the Mediterranean coastal ports.

Strategically, an Iranian instigated Jihad with Turkey joining would mean a battle front nightmare. Assets and shipping lanes within the Persian Gulf, the Gulf of Oman, the Caspian Sea, the Black Sea and the Aegean/ Mediterranean Sea could be targets and would have to be defended. Coastal areas in these bodies of water would also be under threat. The land borders of these two countries poses different threats where Iraq, Pakistan, Afghanistan in the central and Eastern areas and Greece and Bulgaria in the Western area giving a backdoor to the European mainland. Together these two countries would present approximately 6,000 miles of boarders to contain, over 3,100 miles of land boarders and over 2,800 miles of coastal frontage. Iranian missiles launched from the Western reaches of Turkey could reach much of central Europe and everything East of an approximate ark from Marseilles in Southern France, through Geneva and up past and including Berlin.

If oil production was the primary target of such an alliance, then 4 million bpd could be turned off 'in-house', that is 3 million from Iran and 1 million that is piped from Northern Iraq through Turkey to the Mediterranean. An additional 15 million bpd of oil production could be highly threatened in the Gulf and the Caspian requiring major military assets employed for their protection. Such an alliance would also generate the capacity to raise a multi-million man military.

Turkey is the key to the Iranian instigated Jihad. Without Turkey, Iranian ambitions are confined to the regional level. With Turkey, the Jihad stands a chance of reaching that critical mass that will result in a global war of Moslem against Christian. Turkey has for years had a secular military with strong ties to the US. But as the Turkish Parliament moves ever closer to being fully dominated by Moslem parties we can expect to see a more sympathetic military for the government. Slowly but surely the Moslem factions in Parliament are gaining the support of the general population. The Moslem dominated parliament is adept and is determined with its long range planning and patience. The After an investigation into an attempted coup Parliament recently 'traded off' charges against the conspirers that would undoubtedly can for the execution of 39 of their higher ranks for replacing key military positions from the top down with those 'acceptable' to the Parliament. The Moslem support is there in the general population but has not yet been galvanized in to taking action. It will take more than a cartoon drawing of Mohammed in some obscure European paper to galvanize the Turkish populations support for a

Moslem cause. But even a single event, if it is the right one, can sway the general population and the military's support to a much more radical Islamic stance. This event has yet to reveal itself. The recent altercations between a Turkish 'charity' shipment and Israel of goods attempting to break the Israeli imposed Gaza embargo stirred the hearts of many in the Middle East and has gone a long way in mending the public image of Turkey within the Moslem World. Turkey is moving away from its fanciful ambitions of being part of the Western world and more towards the dominant Islamic countries in the region. They will join the Jihad. It is written.

EGYPT

Egypt is the most populous Arab country with about 75 million people mostly on a river and its delta. Most Arab states have a large contingent of Egyptians working within them. Though it professes to be a democracy, it is not. Elections are rigged on a massive scale often entailing the swapping out of ballot boxes that would make any Western politician green with envy. The country is run by the President and the military, of which many officers have been trained by the US. It receives billions of dollars worth of military aid from the US, second only to Israel. Its President and military fit snuggly within the folds of the US Middle East policy on most issues and the rest of the Middle East countries know it all too well.

For years, impoverished Egypt had its hand out to the richer Arab countries, Saudi Arabia in particular. Egypt had lost the Sinai to the Israelis in the 1967 War and had vowed to regain the Sinai. In 1973 Egypt under Sadat, with Soviet weapons bought with Arab money, recaptured The Sinai. Since the 1973 Arab Israeli War, the Saudi money came with more strings attached. For example, if Egypt wanted to buy military equipment worth five billion dollars but could only commit to four billion, then the Saudis might give them the additional one billion dollars with the stipulation that the contracts would go through Saudi designated agents and be awarded to the Saudi choice of suppliers. The Saudis would receive their 5% 'fee' on the entire five billion dollars worth of transaction from the suppliers and where applicable, take position in the stock of the supplier if it were publicly traded. The Saudi's would immediately gain 25% on their one billion to line the pockets of the ruling clique plus whatever multiplier from the gains of trading the suppliers stocks while Egypt received just the hardware. Attempts by Egypt to improve their relationship with the richer Arab states could be seen in some of their political actions. When the Shah of Iran lost Iran to Ayatollah Khomeini the Shah became a wanted man by the new Iranian regime. The Iranians pressured any country that attempted to harbor the Shah, including the US. The Shah was one of America's strongest allies in the Middle East, yet the US would not grant him political asylum beyond the medical treatment he required. Egypt stepped up and offered the Shah residency, not out of any love for the Shah, but rather to send a message to the ruling cliques of all the fragile but rich Middle East Kingdoms and Sheikdoms. The message to these rulers: 'Where will you go when it is your time to run? America? Finally President Sadat of Egypt signed a peace deal with Israel, as Egypt was not willing to pay the price of more war. At the time of the signing there was a plan for the Arab Organization for Industry (AOI) which called for the building of a major military industrial complex on the Egyptian Mediterranean coast to manufacture weaponry for much of the Arab World. This multi-billion dollar enterprise, backed by the Saudis and others, was scraped with the signing of the Egypt/Israel peace. The signing of the peace deal also sealed the fate of President Sadat as it made him an enemy of most of the Middle East.

Egypt has a large US military presence and is of strategic military importance. It borders Israel, with which it has made peace. It has large port facilities on the Mediterranean and the Red Sea and most importantly, it has the Suez Canal. Passage through the Suez Canal means that movement of large quantities of equipment, supplies and personnel are possible between the Persian Gulf/Gulf of Oman area and the Mediterranean Sea in days rather than weeks. This also applies to vast quantities of crude oil destined for Europe. The canal will remain under Egyptian/American military control unless there is a very popular uprising in Egypt. Much of the Egyptian population is poor, under educated and virtually powerless against the firm military grip of the Mubarak government.

It would be difficult for the populace to wrench control of the country away from the Mubarak government or whatever government in power assuming that they retained the same controls as Mubarak. Mubarak's son has already been groomed and received some approval from the powers that be for ascension to the Egyptian Presidential throne. Only a very small fraction of the Egyptian population has any arms or explosives and these people are usually engaged in smuggling the same to the Palestinians in Gaza. Any terrorist act against Egypt, and there have been some, is met with the immediate 'rounding up of the usual suspects' and Egypt keeps a long list of suspects.

An Iranian lead Jihad can wreck havoc on the West if it expands through Turkey. Egypt is not necessary for such expansion but would be a welcomed addition to the cause. Should Egypt and the Suez Canal fall to the Jihad, then the ability of the US to move assets between theaters of war would be at a tremendous disadvantage. The vast majority of the US military logistical support on any foreign soil is transported by ships. This applies to operations in the Middle East as well as to the US military presence in the Mediterranean. Without the use of the Suez Canal, the US would face great logistical problems maintaining operations in and between the Mediterranean and Indian Ocean basin theaters.

Egypt's importance may be the Suez and the US military bases in country, however, its vulnerability is the Nile. The 75 million Egyptians are almost all totally dependent upon the Nile. Desalinization plants on some coastal cities may lessen the dependency upon the Nile yet should the 'quality' of the Nile water be affected anywhere North of the Aswan Dam, then Egypt could simply collapse as a nation. Though Egypt is a US backed forced to be reckoned with, it is still a very vulnerable nation. It is a country with a 75 million population controlled by a 'President', his family, friends, and their US trained military. An old Egyptian joke regarding a previous leader goes; Everyday a fellow would buy a newspaper from a street vendor, glace at the front page and throw the paper away immediately. After watching this ritual for weeks the street vendor asked his customer what he was looking for. "The Obituaries" came the reply. "But the Obituaries are in the back page". "Not the one I'm looking for!" This reference to their waiting for a change of leadership still applies to today. In the coming Jihad most of the Egyptians will hear "the Calling" but will be largely powerless to effect the change needed to wrench control away from ruling clique. There will be unrest and dissention in Egypt when the Jihad begins to gather momentum, however it is doubtful if their government will turn radical

Islamic. There may be enough dissention to keep the Egyptian military from full commitment. Only time will tell.

SYRIA

Syria is another Arab country lead by 'friends and family' of President Bashar Al Assad. The ruling clique has a firm grip on the country and has profited from playing against the West in Lebanon, Iraq and against Israel. It hosts a number or radical organizations and funnels funding and weaponry to the same. Though it claims to be ruled by Baathist party doctrine it is little more than a dictatorship. It gave safe haven and passage, for a price, to many of Saddam's regime. Its long porous board with Iraq became a gateway for rebels and weaponry for those wanting to fight the Americans in Iraq. It has close ties with Iran founded on the principle of "The enemy of my enemy is my friend." Its front line with Israel and the loss of the Golan Heights has kept it in the forefront of anti-Israeli efforts. There is little chance that Israel will return the Golan Heights to Syria while the reign of the Assads continues. From the high ground of the Golan Heights, Israel can target and pound the Syrian capital, Damascus, with artillery. Equally threatening the Golan Heights, in Syrian hands would be an unacceptable threat to the security of Israel.

Syria is not one of the rich oil exporting Arab countries. It receives support from Iran including sophisticated Russia weaponry. Syria has supported radical groups in various degrees. It used the Lebanon civil war as an excuse for the years of occupation of Lebanon. Political assassinations in Lebanon smell strongly of Syrian involvement. Syria and its 'associates' have long been linked to anti-American bombings and other acts of terror. There is little chance of reconciliation between Syria and the US short of a total regime change in Syria. Syria cannot afford peace in the Middle East.

In September 2007, the Israelis bombed a facility under construction in the Northeast area of Syria 50 miles from the Iraqi border. The 'facility' looked remarkably similar to a nuclear reactor modeled after the North Korean design. The Israeli commando raid prior to the air attack apparently confirmed North Korean nuclear material. Within days of the attack, all evidence of the demolished building had been removed. By international agreement, the Syrians would have had at least another year or two, during the construction phase, before they were obligated to declare the nuclear facility to the international nuclear authorities. But the message wasn't that Israel was not going to allow Syria to have a nuclear reactor. The message was to both Iran and Syria and that was; that their air defense systems were penetrable. This is after the Iranians and Syrians had just employed the Russia Pantsyr-S1 system, touted as unjammable by the Russians. It is the latest short-range mobile air defense system that the Russians are selling and suppose to be the best in the world. During the air raid, there were some reports in Syria of electronic interference with many electrical systems, including cell phones being affected. Obviously, the US has made great gains in electronic warfare. Syria had taken delivery of 12 Pantsir-S1 batteries and was due to receive another 24 and Iran even more. The air raid served notice to Iran that they are not prepared to engage the US and expect to inflict heavy casualties on its aircraft. The raid deep into Syrian territory has bought time for the US, Israel and the Gulf states to make final preparations before the US strikes a crushing blow to Iran's nuclear program and offensive capability. Syria could well be included in such an attack. Whether pre-emptive or in retaliation for an Iranian aggressive act, the US will strike Iran. That is also written.

LIBYA

Libya is a large desert country with a small population of about six million. It will be of importance in the coming hostilities, not so much because of the oil it exports, but rather because of its strategic position on the Southern Mediterranean coast. Its leader, Moammar Khaddafi, has made somewhat of an accepted comeback in Western circles. The West had ostracized him for his support and involvement in terrorism. In recent years he took responsibility for the Pan Am bombing over Lockerbie, Scotland and paid restitution to the relatives of the victims. He voluntarily gave up his chemical and biological weapons programs. He was also blamed for the bombing of a night club in Germany that resulted in the deaths of some US servicemen that would frequent the establishment. This act prompted Ronald Reagan to retaliate with an air strike that targeted Khaddafi. Khaddafi was not in the targeted tent at the time of the attack but some of his family members were and died as a result. It was later found out that the Syrians, not the Libyans, were behind the night club bombing in Germany.

Libya's 1200 mile coast and being next to both Tunisia and Egypt would be a welcomed addition to any Jihad, particularly an Iranian backed effort. It would not take too much convincing for Khaddafi to join as he has a very personal score to settle with the US. The Libyan military, though not particularly large or advanced, could pose a real threat in the Mediterranean basin. There are the obvious military possibilities such as disrupting shipping or opening up a new front with Egypt. However, Libya as a party to the Jihad would pose different threats. One threat could be that Iranian missiles launched from Libya or Libyan ships in the Mediterranean could reach many, if not most European cities. Perhaps the greatest threat lies in that Libya has the capability to launch a large pre-emptive strike force to many Southern Europe's coastal cities. Even before the time comes for choosing sides, Libya will quietly be part of the Jihad and possibly the launch point for the initial attack onto European soil.

THE GULF

The rest of the Gulf States, Kuwait, Bahrain, Qatar and the UAE will follow the Saudi lead and their rulers will ally themselves with the US against Iran. Though each state has its own unique character, collectively their importance is the oil that they export. Some, like the UAE depend almost entirely on the Strait of Hormuz for their exports (approx. 90%), hence the massive six plus billion dollar effort to reroute the oil through pipelines to the Gulf of Oman and Yanbu on the Red Sea. Other Gulf States are working with the Saudis to have the option to pipe their oil westward rather than depend upon the stability of the twelve mile wide Strait of Hormuz. Within each of the Gulf States there is a minority segment of the population that is Shiite and undoubtedly small groups of radical elements. For the most part these elements pose little threat; however, there is always the 'Golden BB' factor where the highly unlikely can happen. Militarily, these States have begun to work together under the GCC. Some have purchased high-tech weaponry from the US while others have extended the use of their land for US bases. All will lend whatever logistical support required to the US against any Iranian action.

The vulnerability of the oil infrastructure in the Gulf is great as development of offshore rigs, loading terminals and onshore facilities did not evolve with defensive considerations as a priority. To defend against these vulnerabilities requires massive anti-missile capabilities over hundreds of potential targets and the total command of the Gulf. Total command of the Gulf means the ability to annihilate all watercraft as they depart the Iranian shoreline and keep the skies free of enemy aircraft and missiles. Larger naval vessels offer excellent targets and should not pose a problem after the first thirty minutes of a US strike. The thousands of small craft pose a much more serious problem as the sheer number of craft covering such an expanse of water means that some may be able to find temporary lapses in security allowing mines to be laid, missiles to be fired or suicide missions to be conducted. The Iranians have a new class of small submarines much more suitable for the shallow waters of the Gulf. The effectiveness of these new submarines are difficult to evaluate especially considering the US ability in anti-submarine warfare.

In the Gulf, the real issue is who attacks first. If the Iranians launched a massive pre-emptive attack, then they could wreck havoc on most of the oil production and transportation in the region, closing the Gulf and halting production of most of the oil in the region for at least a year or two. If the US attacks first, with a massive campaign, then Iran and its ability to retaliate would be greatly diminished. The Gulf will turn red with blood, that much is written.

THE CLOCK

President Bush had made it clear that he considered Iran a very real and present threat. An Iran with nuclear weapons is totally unacceptable to Israel, the US and several European nations, whether they admit it publicly or not. Saudi Arabia and the rest of the Gulf states would have to capitulate to any and all demands of a nuclear Iran. Western public opinion and support for an attack against Iran's nuclear capability can be influenced overnight and certainly within the course of a month. Satellite pictures, intercepted communications or the defection of a high ranking official that reveals detailed intelligence of an Iranian nuclear weapons program that are made public would all but seal Iran's fate. Leaks of a secret program could even come from third parties such as Pakistan or North Korea. Demands for immediate cessation, comprehensive monitoring and total unfettered access to any and all suspected sites could be made with immediate deadlines and immediate consequences for non-compliance. Any or all of these 'influences' could spring into the public arena at any time. However, even if such information were known it would be far more prudent to prepare for the probable confrontation before going public. These types of revelations can easily trigger the start of armed conflict or there can be steadily increasing rhetoric amongst the parties over a period of several months. The obvious advantage of 'revelations' over rhetoric in fulfilling an agenda is the urgency factor. A public's reaction or over reaction to a 'revelation' can empower a government to take swift action, even without thorough validation of the facts.

A 'revelation' can be used to diffuse an escalating situation until suitable preparations are in place. For example, if the Iranians were preparing a massive pre-emptive strike before the US and the Gulf States were fully prepared then a 'revelation' such as an intelligence report that claims that Iran discontinued its nuclear weapons ambitions in 2003 would go a long way to diffusing the immediate tensions. A 'revelation' used in such a manner can easily be reversed and justified to the public at the appropriate time.

In the case of Iran, the validation of the facts for the benefit of the public is not of high priority. The administrations of both Israel and the US seem predetermined to carry out a military action against Iran. Regardless of whatever US Administration intentions or desire of the future may now be, Iran has been made an enemy of the US and Israel since the beginning of the Regan era. A 'revelation' of Iran's nuclear weapons ambitions would not need to be validated to a great extent before military action began. It does not really matter whether or not Iran is actually developing nuclear weapons. In all likelihood they probably have some secret program working diligently towards nuclear weapons. What matters is that Israel and the US administrations are intent on reducing Iran's military capacity.

There are several considerations that influence the timing of a US strike against Iran. First and foremost is Iran's pace of advancement. This applies to conventional and non-conventional weapons and its military industry as a whole. Iran's nuclear program has been spread out to scores of locations with some evidence that suggests that it may be as high as 300 locations. Granted, many of these operations are probably duplicated several times to increase the survivability chances of critical operations in the event of an attack. But this is not the logical planning of a regime that's after nuclear power for peaceful purposes. It just is not. It is the planning of a regime hell bent on a nuclear program that it feels must survive any initial assault or have such comprehensive backup that would discourage attempts to thwart its progress by military action. Such planning, costs and risks do not justify the benefits of conventional nuclear power production and makes even less since for a country exporting three million barrels of oil a day. The only logical conclusion is that Iran is working on a nuclear weapons program.

Given that Iran is on the path to nuclear weapons, then we have to take a quick look at its fundamental nuclear capacity to evaluate the time frame before they can begin production. First, Iran has raw uranium in the ground so there is no limitation to the raw material needed to refine the ore into suitable concentrates. Second, many centrifuges are required to refine the ore. Usually in a cascading configuration where the uranium is centrifuged in a hexafluoride gas to slightly concentrate the uranium. This slightly concentrated product is again centrifuged to concentrate it even more, again and again until the desired concentration is reached. Nuclear reactors require about 40% concentration but would require massive amounts of high explosives, probably an oil supertanker worth, to create the chain reaction that goes 'big-a-bang'. The greater the concentration the less you need for 'critical mass' and the less of a trigger you need to initiate the chain reaction. As you approach the 90% range then you can weaponize a warhead of a missile. Concentration percentages in the high nineties gives you the 'briefcase bomb'. Iran has committed vast sums of money to cascade their ore. They have purchased what centrifuges they could and are manufacturing their own centrifuges. Even giving that their centrifuges may not be up to performance standard of Western centrifuges, they still refine the ore, and they just may need more centrifuges or more time. Iran has produced thousands of centrifuges and continues to produce more. This is what they have publicly disclosed and verified by the UN inspectors. If Iran has a large scale secret nuclear program as opposed to a limited one, then it is conceivable that these thousands of centrifuges are only a fraction of the true number that they now possess and continue to build. If such were the case, then they would quickly develop the capacity to produce at least a dozen nuclear weapons if not more per year. This is the most critical determining factor of the timing of the 'first strike', either by the US or Iran. Lack of detailed intelligence would induce Israel and the US to estimate on the shorter end of the possible time frame. Whatever intelligence the US and Israel have would most probably be incomplete and again encourage errs to the shorter time frame.

The second determining factor of the timing of a US strike on Iran would be the military preparedness of the US, Israel and the Gulf States. The military preparedness must be the capacity to repel any counter attack whether it is from aircraft, missile, marine, land based or other, such as terror cells. The US has the military presence in Iran's immediate vicinity to commence and maintain an assault campaign that, if pre-emptive, would greatly reduce Iran's capacity to conduct almost anything, let alone a conventional counter offensive. However, I doubt that any US general would be willing to 'guarantee' that not a single missile, aircraft, speedboat or other assault against the highly flammable Gulf targets would not get through. And, if one missile or speed boat can get through the defenses, then it's conceivable that two, three, four or more could get through. Given more time, the US and Gulf States can strengthen its anti-missile defense coverage, make ready better defensive measure to protect the oil infrastructure and devise plans to try to hold Iran to its own shores. Preparations for a massive sustained assault requires vast amounts of logistics in place at the onset of hostilities. Troop rotations, ordinance, fuel and supplies all have to be at their peak or optimum levels for the best chance of success.

Then comes the difficult question of which side is strengthening their position more effectively as time progresses. This is a fluid question as most of the variables are in a constant state of flux. But there comes a point of diminished returns if one side is to use the advantage of a pre-emptive strike. And, at some point in time, it may be possible to catch the opposition in a vulnerable state. Choosing this window of opportunity can be dependent upon intelligence, and in particular, satellite intelligence, of which the US has a tremendous advantage. These factors combined suggest that if a US decision to go to war was made on say January 1st, 2011, then it may take six months or more to achieve optimum readiness, particularly if it is to be done without raising the suspicions of the other side.

Then the next consideration would be for alternative transportation of crude oil in the event of the closure, even if temporary, of the Strait of Hormuz. In the latter half of 2007 plans began to surface in the Western press that indicated that the Gulf States were serious about by-passing the Strait of Hormuz. Some pipelines from the UAE would go overland to the Gulf of Oman and some would tie into the Saudi pipeline network to Yanbu on the Red Sea coast. Similar efforts of the other Gulf States and double digit billions of dollars being committed means that the Arab Gulf States take very serious the possibility of Iran closing the Strait. Exact plans, routes, capacities and construction schedules are sensitive to say the least.

The fact that work has already commenced on bypassing the Strait says volumes. To the Iranians it says that the entire Gulf has chosen sides and will not be intimidated by the possible closure of the Strait. It also puts the Iranian leverage over the Strait on a timetable. If the Iranians want to close the Strait while it will still affect the flow of oil from the Gulf, and if they do so before they are attacked, then they will suffer the condemnation of an oil thirsty world with the possible exception of Russia who would profit greatly by such an act. By bypassing the Strait, it also reverses the advantage and puts Iran on the clock. When the Arab oil in the Gulf no longer has to pass through the Strait of Hormuz to reach market, then the US or the Gulf States could close the Strait and cause the Iranians problems with their oil exports. Towards the latter half of 2011 the strategic value of the Strait will begin to shift in favor of the US/Arab Gulf States. It seems unlikely and unnecessary for either side to begin an all out military campaign during the first half of 2011. It may seem that the logical option for Iran would be to attack while such an action would have maximum disruption to the flow of oil, but there are other considerations. Any military action would most certainly cause the cessation of deliveries of Russian nuclear fuel for the first nuclear reactor in Iran. As of January 2008 the Iranians have received three of the eight deliveries of fuel with deliveries scheduled to be completed by the summer of 2008. Any military action would most probably include a US strike against most of the Iranian nuclear program. And every week that goes by without military engagement means another couple of billion dollars or so that Iran can apply to their cause. At the start of 2010, neither side is as ready as they would like to be.

The Israelis have serious time considerations. They have to have the US attack Iran. If Israel were to attack Iran on its own and targeted anything other than the nuclear reactor and elements critical to their program then they risk the possibility of inciting the entire Moslem World against them. Israel would risk this if it were to prevent Iran from obtaining a nuclear warhead, let alone the capacity to produce a few warheads a year. The US cannot risk another Arab Israeli war that would most certainly see oil used as a weapon. The US will be the frontline to challenge Iran. Every month that goes by, the Iranians get closer to their objective. Israel will demand that Iran be engaged before they achieve nuclear weapons production. Bush had already made repeated statements publicly regarding the danger of Iran and how it cannot be allowed nuclear weapons. President Obama has indicated the same resolve. Should Iran even obtain one or two warheads from a third party, then they have the capacity to threaten Israel. Of course Israel has anti missile batteries. But with a determined enemy, Israel may be faced with wave after wave of decoy missiles until its capacity to intercept is diminished. Again, this would be an unacceptable option for Israel, and thus the US. The crux of the whole issue comes down to the 'determined enemy', in this case the ruling religious clique in Iran. This is not about President Ahmedinajad as he was allowed to serve by the Guardian Council and other religious bodies that make up Iran's 'board of directors' who's chairman of the board is Ayatollah Khatamie, the Supreme Leader. Ahmedinajad can be instantly dismissed from his duties should he meet with disapproval of Khatamie or the other non-elected religious institutions, even executed with the wave of a hand by the all mighty Ayatollah. This is the real power in Iran and it holds a firm grip on the country. A massive attack on Iran's military may significantly reduce their capacity to retaliate; however, it would not diminish the resolve of the religious extremists that grip the country so tightly.

Iran continues racing towards nuclear weapons production while the US prepares to stop it, dead in its tracks. This is no longer a diplomatic matter as the courses are set in stone. Iran wants nuclear weapons and Israel, via the US, is going to deny them that privilege.

Let's be clear that it is Israel's desires that Iran does not get nuclear weapons is the main push in this instance. America was the first nation to produce atomic and nuclear weapons and used them on Japan. The USSR was quick to follow. Though tensions were high between the two the US and USSR never went to all out war between each other. They did usher in the 'Cold War' with lots of chest pounding and nuclear testing, but never direct confrontation. China was scared that its antagonistic neighbor had nuclear weapons so somehow they obtained the knowhow to produce their own. The US, nor china, nor the USSR engaged in nuclear war. England and France obtained membership to the nuclear club but because they were smart, responsible and defensive about the matter nobody seemed to protest. But India's neighbor, China had nuclear weapons so India felt compelled to join the club, and so they did. Pakistan, India's neighbor and rival felt that it needed to level out the playing field between the two and gained membership to the nuclear club. Not since Hiroshima and Nagasaki has anyone anywhere used atom or nuclear weaponry against another nation. South Africa joined the club but withdrew their membership by their own volition. North Korea has some nuclear weapons of sorts but they are just too poor to produce any real quality merchandise of any kind. Israel, of course, has nuclears, but it is 'accepted' that they need it as a deterrent. That means that it is sort of 'accepted' by the rest of the nuclear club that Israel will 'nuke' any and all Middle East countries that it becomes militarily engaged with, that it cannot defeat or hold off with conventional weapons. None of these members of the nuclear club have dropped a bomb on their enemy for one simple fact. The rest of the world would condemn them and retaliation from other members of the elite club could be swift, total and demanded. Take for a hypothetical example Pakistan using a nuclear device on an Indian city. No one would condemn Indian for a nuclear retaliation. Once you open that Pandora's Box you go all the way, so there would go Pakistan with a couple of hundred million people, give or take a few million. Enemies Pakistan and India may be enemies, however they have refrained from using nuclear weapons, even using the threat of nuclear weapons, knowing perhaps that the first one that breaks the 'no nukes' rule will be annihilated by others. So why the absolute refusal to let Iran join the 'Club'? This is really the crux of the whole matter leading up to World War III and the coming Jihad so I will actually repeat the question. Why, why the absolute refusal to let Iran join the 'Club'? Iran manufactures its own missiles now that can reach parts of Europe but have not used them. They have launched a satellite into low orbit and working on a three stage rocket that can put a satellite or whatever else into an orbit 600 miles above. They certainly must know that a missile attack on Israel or American interests in the region would spell their total and absolute destruction. Iran can and could have closed the Strait of Hormuz 'by accident' with one, two or three of their own ships sunk at the precise strategic point that blocks any oil tanker of size from passage, yet they have not. Again, perhaps they have not because they know it would spell their immediate and total doom. Why not let them go nuclear and force them to uphold the responsibility that comes with such power? Every other member of the nuclear club understands that, so why not just let them obtain membership? The answer is simple, Israel. Whether you believe it or not Israel has conducted such atrocities against the Palestinian population it would and has been convicted for crimes against humanity time and time again except that the US systematically 'Vetoes' every one of the multitude of General Assembly votes against Israel. The entire Middle East despises Israel, their horrific treatment of the Palestinians and America's unquestioning defense of Israel. It is a painful and boring process to recount the oh so numerous United Nations sanctions against Israel that have been 'vetoed' by the US. The United Nations avenue of recourse, justice or equitable settlement for the Palestinians is totally mute thanks to the Israeli 'influence' over the US political machine. However, a nuclear capable Iran would by-pass the US defunked processes and force Israel to give the Palestinians a 'Homeland' unless they wanted a 'Nuclear War'. If Iran could deliver even 10 square miles of a real Palestinian state, then they win, they win the hearts and minds of 90% of the Middle East population and that is far more than necessary for the critical mass of support required to effect sweeping changes. That prospect is just not acceptable to Israel as they are still in their land-acquisition mode. Some of the Israeli hard liners believe that 'Israel' should be 'from the Euphrates to the Nile' as written in the Old Testament. A nuclear capable

Iran could also dominate the entire Gulf region. This is an unacceptable option as it is clear that Iran is now unfortunately an enemy of the US with irreconcilable differences.

The sides are chosen and each side is not even looking for peace. Both sides are quietly and not so quietly preparing for military confrontation, which means War in layman's terms. The fuse is definitely lit with Iran's nuclear ambitions. That much they have written. The question is not whether or not war will erupt, rather when, where and what type of war?

LESSONS LEARNED

For decades the Middle East has been a hotbed of activity that engaged many powers, both East and West. The 1967 Arab Israeli War, the 1968 Baathist Coup in Iraq, Colonel Khaddafi, Saddam Hussein, The Shah, Ayatollah Khomeini, the 1973 Arab Israeli War and oil embargo, the Lebanon Civil War, Iraq invasion of Kuwait, the first Gulf War, the Syrian occupation of Lebanon, the occupation of Iraq and countless other events now fill the history books of the region. Include 'Nine-Eleven', Afghanistan and Pakistan and there is plethora of lessons that have been learned by even the most casual observer in the region. Some of the more notable lessons that have surfaced from the Middle East will impact the coming Jihad.

The US Embassy Hostage Crisis in Tehran and again in Beirut taught the Middle East the real value of a hostage and in particular a Western hostage. In the case of the embassy hostages, it rendered a superpower powerless. It was an important contributing factor in the US elections that brought a change of administration. It also forced the US to make a desperate and unsuccessful military rescue attempt. In the case of Beirut it proved that even the US could be reduced to negotiating with hostage takers. For their 'assistance' in helping to secure the release of the hostages in Beirut, Iran received sophisticated shoulder fired weapons that could easily down an Iraqi helicopter or destroy a tank. This 'Iran-Contra' deal, when it became public, caused Saddam to retaliate with an Exocite missile strike upon the USS Stark, killing a few dozen US crewmen. During the first Gulf War the value of taking a city hostage was learned. The Iraqi troops were virtually untouched while they occupied Kuwait City but were decimated upon their retreat. Indeed, Kuwait City itself was virtually untouched by the US while it was occupied. Syria's occupation of Lebanon was the taking of a country hostage. It gave Syria the added protection that any actions against Syria could also be paid for by Lebanon. The breakup of the former Yugoslavia and Saddam during the first Gulf war saw the use of Hostages as human shields. Hostage taking in the Middle East has been tried and tested in various forms from common kidnappers for cash ransoms, to fringe radical groups wanting to make a political statement of global impact, to governments battling via proxy wars, to human shields used to defend vital interests. Hostage taking in the Middle East has matured in to an integral part of any strategy of consequence.

Another lesson learned is conventional warfare is for conventional battlefields, not for civilian environments. In conventional warfare in an open battlefield environment, it is technology, training and tactics that win the day. And, the US is the undeniable king of conventional warfare. In the 1973 Arab Israeli war the Egyptians employed the technology, training and tactics designed specifically to combat the established and fixed Israeli technology, training and tactics and they won back the Suez Canal. The engineers in the Egyptian Army used water cannons to wash down the high sand embankments of the Bar-Lev line that the Israelis erected to stop any armored advance. They also erected pontoon bridges across the Canal over which their armor crossed. Knowing that the Israelis would send their Air force to destroy the bridges, the Egyptians operated under the protective cover of long-range and short-range Surface-to-Air Missiles (SAM 6 and 7s). The Israelis sped their tanks forward to meet the advancing armor only to meet Egyptian infantry armed with shoulder fired TOW wire-guided missiles. In this case, the Egyptians employed the technology, training and tactics to specifically combat known technology training and tactics of their adversary. It demonstrated that there are always chinks in the armor. It also rules out conventional warfare on an open battlefield against US armed forces. However, the new battlefield of war also includes public opinion. The US withdrew from Viet Nam, not because of superior armed forces or unsustainable losses. The US had far superior weaponry and was inflicting casualty damage at a ratio of at least twenty to one. The US withdrew because of their domestic public opinion. The US has faced mounting negative public opinion over its occupation of Iraq encouraged by elements around the world that wanted to see the US fail and retreat from Iraq. Propaganda is the weapon of choice and the battleground is the media the world over. This includes the internet, a battleground whose terrain is morphing and difficult to navigate. The internet gives a new dimension to the propaganda war. It empowers users to instantly disseminate information around the globe. It can offer anonymous training in tactics, weapon use and manufacture and identify potential targets and do so in a relatively safe virtual environment. It can offer a means to transmit coded messages and communications in real time. And it offers a platform for the written word, pictures and video to fan the flames of a movement. Increasingly, the propaganda wars are gaining importance as the ultimate battle for the hearts and minds of men rages.

Guerilla tactics and terror work and work particularly well in large urban environment were proximity of civilians and conventional armed forces is close and constant. For years the Palestinians have engaged the Israelis at arm's length by firing their short range missiles into the Israeli held lands. This requires that Israel maintain a large military presence in and near these areas. Israel's military has a large contingent of part-timers or civilians that can be called up quickly in time of need. These tactics are designed to fight a war of attrition and demoralize the local populations. During the Civil War in Lebanon guerilla warfare and terror tactics became common place and refined because it was the most effective way to demoralize and strike fear in the enemy. In Iraq, it was used to thwart US and Iraqi government control and used effectively to force a high price for the US to operate in that environment. IED's, sniper fire and booby traps made even the most menial tasks in Iraq a life threatening proposition. The use of small arms and rocket propelled grenades only compound the problem. With the use of 'hit and run' guerilla tactics and with remote control detonation of explosives, small numbers of rebels can force the opposition to maintain a large force to protect many potential targets. Targeting infrastructures such as electricity or fuel distribution can bring a country to a virtual standstill and show that an enemy is unworthy to govern. Guerilla warfare is most effective when the instigators can fade into the civilian population for cover. The use of terror is often used as a threat against a civilian population to maintain that cover.

Suicide bombers bring a new dimension to warfare. Most of our human activity has evolved without considering the threat of a suicide bomber and consequently many vulnerabilities are now having to be dealt with. We are all familiar with airport screenings where passengers and their baggage have to pass security checks. But most of our human activity is vulnerable to a suicide bomber attack. Simple activities that Western countries take for granted such as going to an open air market, a movie theater, a mall, a wedding, a funeral, a school, in short, any gathering of people are potential targets. Additionally, there are static, non human targets that are of critical importance. All are vulnerable to a suicide bomber.

Oil has been used successfully in warfare. In the 1973 Arab Israeli War the Arab oil exporters quadrupled their prices and threaten an oil embargo against any country that helped Israel. After Saddam invaded Kuwait he used oil as both a carrot and a stick. He offered the US cheap oil but did not fathom the US's true intentions. Saddam then had the Kuwaiti oil fields set a blaze, but not before he tried to pump millions of barrels into the Gulf. In today's oil thirsty world oil has become of the utmost importance. The oil in the Gulf will be the target in the coming Jihad. Double digit billions of dollars are being spent to safeguard it's delivery. If Iran can deny the Gulf oil to the rest of the world then it has leverage against being attacked by the US. The Gulf States are working furiously to reroute its oil exports away from the dependency of using the Strait of Hormuz to transport their oil because the Strait are just too difficult to secure. Though all the Arab Gulf oil may be able to be rerouted in the coming year or two, it does not change the fact that most of the oil produced in the region is in or immediately adjacent to the Gulf. Oil platforms, derricks, pumping stations and even pipelines are fixed static targets and highly flammable. Oil will be the primary target in the coming Jihad.

There are many chinks in the armor of the West and Middle East. Vulnerabilities abound simply because most of our human activity did not evolve incorporating defensive measures into their basic design. Oil derricks were not designed with armor clad siding to protect against RPG or missile strikes. Our sidewalks and building entrances are not lined with monitoring devices that can detect explosive components. And there are many new tactics and technologies that can be employed to exploit these weaknesses. Biological and chemical weapons have been around for decades and are relatively easy for a committed government to make. No matter what defensive measures may be taken, there will always exist vulnerabilities that can be exploited.

As of the beginning of 2010, tensions between Iran and the US seem to have eased a bit with the publication of a US Intelligence Report that claims that Iran had discontinued its nuclear weapons ambitions in 2003. This was a timely release as Iranian speed boats began to challenge US naval vessels passing through the Strait of Hormuz. It seemed that the Iranians were challenging the US to open conflict and doing so right in the section of the Strait that is only 12 miles wide. In essence the Iranians were sending the message "You want to fight? How about right here, right now?". So it was very very extremely convenient that the Intelligence Report came out when it did as it gave a face saving pretense for the Americans to publicly back down and have the Iranians do the same. It seemed that the pressure was off as the US's own Intelligence Report negated suspicions that the Iranians were after nuclear weapons. But the US continues to spearhead international efforts to increase sanctions against Iran for their possible pursuit of nuclear weapon material. These efforts include pressuring Russia and China, both allies of Iran, to backing harsher sanctions against Iran by means of a UN Security Council resolution. The US has the support of many of its European allies, including France, Germany and England, in mounting pressure against Iran. But why would the US increase pressure on Iran when the Intelligence Report claims that Iran abandoned its quest for nuclear weapons in 2003? Why do the Gulf States continue spending billions of dollars to reroute their oil? Why has the US approved a thirty billion dollar arms package to Israel? Why did President Bush approved tens of billions in sophisticated arms sales to Saudi Arabia and the other Gulf States. Sophisticated American weaponry continues to flood the Middle East and in particular Israel. The only plausible reason that all these actions have transpired in just the past few years is that the threat from Iran is real and eminent. Why is military action from Iran eminent? The only plausible answer would be in retaliation for a US attack. There may be other factors that become public or events that transpire that would cause hostilities between Iran and the US. However, as it stands now, it seems that the US will destroy Iran's nuclear capacity and most probably its ability to retaliate against the Gulf interest before Iran can fully gain the fruits of their nuclear weapons program. President Obama cannot very well give a time and date, for he might as well include the initial targets. The Iranians know this as well as evidenced by the preparedness to challenge US naval vessels. They have known this for years. The big question is exactly when? The exact date may not be known by any person as of this writing, but the first person to know the exact time, date and targets will be President Obama. It is not unfathomable that among the initial targets will be those that stand a good chance of destabilizing the Iranian government. The ideal scenario from the US's standpoint would be that Iran's nuclear and 'other' targets are taken out during the initial strikes and that prompts a regime change in Iran, to one favorable to the West and it's new governments, embracing the US for its liberation efforts. Just like the US did in Iraq. The big difference between Iraq and Iran being that the Iranian regime is religious based and has a backup military as a safeguard against such an eventuality.
All the parties concern must know what is coming down the line as they are acting accordingly. The US would want to attack as early as possible, that is as soon as they feel that they can guarantee a significant percentage, if not all, of the Gulf States oil supplies to the world. Or, have

the military capability in place to repel any Iranian attempts to disrupt the flow of oil. It is doubtful that that capability would exist before the middle of 2011, however, anytime soon thereafter would be a possible launch date.

If the US strikes Iran in the second half of 2011, the rulers of the Gulf States will publicly be for the US thus isolating Iran politically. The US already has Iran surrounded, literally. The regime in Iran will feel desperate and be forced to take drastic measures. Whether or not Iran will be capable of attacking the oil interests in the Gulf after they have suffered a US attack is yet to be seen. Assuming that they cannot or their ability is very limited then they will attempt to expand the war to force Moslem against Christian worldwide, in essence a Jihad. With a Jihad, Iran stands a chance in that the Moslem countries that did not join, their populations, particularly of the Gulf states would rise up and overthrow the fragile monarchies. If Iran cannot destroy the oil, then perhaps it can still deny it to the West.

The Iranians may attempt to send missiles to Israel in an effort to draw Israel into direct conflict. That would swing the pendulum of sentiment of the Arab populations against Israel and the US. By appealing to the anti-Israeli sentiment of the Arab populations, the Iranians would stand a chance that the respective governments in the Middle East would side with Iran or at least remain neutral. But the chances of Iranian long range missiles surviving the initial US attack would be small. And any missiles that survived and fired at Israel would have to pass the gauntlet of US anti-missile defenses in Iraq and of Israel.

Iran should have received the entire 82 tons of nuclear fuel for its reactor from the Russians. Though nuclear fuel is far lower grade than what is desired for a nuclear weapon, it is a significant head start on the road to enrichment. And with thousand of centrifuges, should Iran 'decide' to develop a nuclear weapon, then it is conceivable that they could produce several in just a few months. At the very least 82 tons of nuclear fuel it is ample material for hundreds of 'dirty bombs'.

Iran can not engage Israel directly in a land war without the participation of Turkey. Iran's ties with Syria cannot be supported logistically for a sustained military campaign against Israel without Turkey. And to engage Israel directly would invite nuclear retaliation by Israel. Iran must find another way to force a Jihad that pits Moslem against Christians. They will need to turn the Christian world against the Moslem world and do so probably in a very weakened state after suffering a US attack. Time will be against the Iranians as a major military action by the US against Iran would undoubtedly include elements of their infrastructure, particularly if the US was trying to encourage regime change. The Iranians must know that for all their attempts at bravado, any serious pre-emptive attack by the US would totally destroy them as a functioning nation. At some point the Iranians will seriously consider a pre-emptive strike of their own.

The Iranians could take some hostages and use them as leverage. But that would not even come close to their objectives. They would have to take thousands upon thousands to have any significant impact on world affairs. They could take a city hostage, but which city? Any city of importance in Iraq already has an active US or Iraqi military presence or has protection zones around it that would preclude such an attempt. Besides, an Iraqi city, any Iraqi city still wouldn't have the desired impact. There are important coastal cities throughout the Gulf but again, to reach these cities the Iranians would have to pass a gauntlet of US naval vessels that could decimate any large scale attempt on a Gulf city. Any city that Iran would target would have to be unprotected and of importance to the West. Iran has a submarine fleet so a surprise attack of a coastal city is not unfathomable. Before nine eleven, such an attack on the US was unfathomable.

The criteria for selecting a target would have to go far beyond its military defenses. The target could be something as simple as a nuclear reactor on the coast of a European shore line, but it is not. It has to have a population base to hold hostage. The hostage factor is all important as it has been proven to bend the will of every US administration. Any city with a population of over one hundred thousand should fit that bill. A city of one million plus would be better. A capital city of a nation would be better still as the ruling government would be most cooperative in securing 'terms' for their eventual release. The city would have to be of great importance. There are an assortment of cities with great economic importance, some with refineries or nuclear reactors or being central hubs of trade and transportation. There are a dozen or so cities in Europe, that, if taken hostage, could bring military retaliation efforts to a screeching halt. London, Paris etc., the European capitals certainly. Some are easily accessible some are not. But there is only one city that would guarantee a Jihad between East and West. And it happens to fit all the criteria for a relatively easy target to take and secure for the few critical hours until unfettered reinforcements could arrive. It is assessable by sea and has the proverbial 'ring road' that can be used to secure exit routes from the city. And most importantly, it is the only city, that if sacked and pillaged, would guarantee a division between East and West, or more accurately, between the Moslem World and the Christian World.

The target city for kick-starting a Jihad would be Rome, specifically, the Vatican. It fits all the necessary criteria. Accessible from the sea, virtually unprotected, has two and a half to three million hostages in the immediate vicinity and is the home of the Vatican, the center of the Catholic faith.

Taking the city of Rome hostage could be done with a small task force that seals off the major exit routes from the city and hold it with the threat of biologicals or chemicals until reinforcements could arrive, a matter of only a few hours if planned correctly. No Western government would condemn two million plus hostages, including the Pope and all the sitting Cardinals just to root out a couple of thousand of the enemy task force, certainly not President Obama. The threat of biologicals of chemicals upon a city of two million or more is an occurrence to which the West has not been tested. In the US battles with Iraq, it was communicated to the Iraqis that if they used chemical or biological weapons then the US would not hesitate to go nuclear. Special consideration would have to be given to Rome due to the fact that Rome surrounds the Vatican City. Nuking Rome would certainly not be an option. And would the US sink a troop transport ship carrying a few thousand reinforcements and seal the fate of two million Italians, including all those in the Vatican? Italy would certainly not allow it. Again, we have seen hostages used with great results in the Middle East, most notably with the US Embassy in Tehran and the Western hostages in Beirut. Cities can and have taken hostage as with Kuwait City and again, with great results for the hostage takers. A country has even been taken hostage as with the Syrian occupation of Lebanon. Rome would be the ideal target for the greatest impact for the least amount of effort.

Considering the environment during which such a move on Rome would be made gives us a clearer picture of the probability of such an act. Whether Iran initiates this action as a pre-emptive 'first strike' because they feel the imminent threat from the US or it is in retaliation for a US strike against Iran's nuclear program does matter to a degree, however, the end result will still be the same. The US will attack the Iranian nuclear program, totally decimating it. Any such attack would almost certainly be accompanied with a sustained attack on the Iranian military capability to retaliate. Such an attack would last for a few days at the very least and possible for a week or two as targets of opportunity continued to present themselves. During this assault on Iran tens of thousands, if not hundreds of thousands of Iranians would die, many of them innocent women and children. The propaganda war would be thrown into high gear on both sides, with Iran playing the tune of the Zionist/US plot to annihilate the Moslem World. These claims would be in conjunction with images and video on the internet and other sources that show the atrocities that the 'Zionist/US alliance' would be committing. It would not fall upon deaf ears as for three generations there has been a plethora of anti-Zionist rhetoric filling the Moslem media. The 'Call' would go out for a Jihad and through prudence, all Western countries would be forced to keep a very close eye on their Moslem populations. Phone calls, emails and other communications would be monitored and any 'suspicious' characters would probably be rounded up for 'questioning' or their own protection as with the Japanese population in the US during World War II. All these activities would be more fuel for the fires of the Jihad. The taking hostage of Rome would force an issue worldwide. It would cause most, if not all, nations of the world to choose sides. Each nation would have to declare publicly in no uncertain terms on whose side they were and the steps they would offer in the aftermath. The Kingdoms and Sheikdoms in the Gulf region would be in a most precarious position. On the one hand they have allied themselves with the US and their rulers have all distanced themselves from Iran. But when the Jihad reaches a critical mass, then it will be perceived that these rulers are siding with Israel and against Islam. Most of these countries rule with an iron fist but at some point their military will question their rulers actions against Islam. If one ruling family bolts out of country for safety then there could be the domino effect that spreads throughout the Gulf. Be sure that rumors of vacating the thrown will fly as well as attempts be made to force the removal of these monarchs. The mood of the populations will be affected by the propaganda war that will be waged. Much will depend upon the level of destruction that the US brings to Iran. That the US will strike Iran is in little doubt, but there are attacks and then there are attacks. If the US were to target just Iran's nuclear reactor and say half a dozen sites that were most critical to its nuclear program then it would be a clear case of no nukes for Iran. Then, on the other hand, the US targets 150 sites related to their nuclear program, every aircraft (military and non-military), every missile battery, every naval vessel that it can find and even the various ruling Councils and some critical infrastructure such as power, water, communications, in short every target of value that could be used against the US or oil facilities in the Gulf basin., then there will be little doubt that the US intentions are to cast Iran back to the stone age. In such a scenario, Iranian casualties could reach 100,000 in the first week or two as many of the targets would be surrounded by a populace of sorts. Shiite or Sunni wouldn't matter as it would be view as an assault on Islam. In the event of such a wide spread attack the road would be cleared for Syria and possibly Libya to immediately join the Jihad. Syria would join in any case as it knows that it is not and cannot be in the good graces of the US so long as the present regime rules. Again, for the Jihad to break out of the Gulf theater and gain traction elsewhere, it needs Turkey to join their cause. Turkey would give Iran unfettered access to the Mediterranean. The Mediterranean basin would also be critical to the Jihad as a weapon against Israel. If a city, any European coastal city, can be taken and held hostage for a few hours until reinforcements arrive, by the use or threat of use of biologicals or chemicals, then why not the neighboring city? And the one next to that? And the one next to that? On and on until this pattern becomes a strategy. A strategy for which there is no defense. If one million hostages, including the Vatican City, are taken in the city of Rome and are used successfully as leverage for the protection of the mass of reinforcements that will arrive hours later, then where does this strategy end? What leader in Europe or the US would trade the annihilation of the Vatican, the Pope and a million or two Italians for 5,000 reinforcements, that would be an easy target, on the high seas? Five thousand heavily armed soldiers could lock down the main conduits out of the city until the next wave of twenty thousand reinforcements arrive. The twenty odd thousand could lock up the city until the next two hundred thousand arrive safely to their various destinations to expand and replicate the strategy. Just as the Egyptians had devised a strategy against the Israelis in October, 1973 that played upon the vulnerabilities, the Iranians, indeed the whole Middle East has watched and learned the value that the West places upon hostages.

If you extend this strategy that you can take a city on the Mediterranean coast and replicate the tactic hundreds of times then it is conceivable that you could gain control of the entire Mediterranean coast. But why is the Mediterranean coast so important to a Jihad against Israel and the US? Simply because, if you control the Mediterranean coast, then you control all the shipping within and that means that Israel would be isolated.

An isolated Israel could not survive. An Israel surrounded by a few hundred miles of hostile air and sea would spell the end of Israel by attrition. At that point, even if Israel nuked fifty cities in the Middle East it would not stop the blockade. Especially if all the Jihad warriors are engaged in European coastal cities and islands. This would not be a duplication of the Berlin airlift as Israel is far from self-sufficient and requires vast amounts of everything to survive. Airlifts would have to pass through hundreds of miles of hostile airspace. Shipments of fuel, food and the tens of billions of dollars worth of weaponry Israel receives every year from the US would stop or certainly be reduced to a trickle. Though Israel manufactures much of its critical and basic weaponry, all the raw materials come from aboard. A war of attrition against Israel could be fought on the shores of the Mediterranean without firing a single shot into Israel. This whole strategy of taking Mediterranean coastal cities hostage may seem farfetched to the average Westerner but is child's play and the only logical option to those in the Middle East that have spent fifty or more years contemplating alternatives. Just as the West knows that an attack on the city of Mecca would infuriate the Moslem World, likewise, the Middle East understand that an assault on the Vatican would have similar effects.

The effect of targeting Rome and the Vatican as the first primary target, the Jihad gains the ultimate power of the 'hostage'. The Pope is not just a man or mascot, but the highest Christian human link to God and as such it is the Pope that holds high the flag of Christianity.

To assault the Vatican and the Pope would be an assault on all Christianity. To hold them hostage would be to hold hostage the faith of every Christian nation. Catholic, Protestant, Baptist and every other fragment of Christian faith will be instantly galvanized as one, unified in a common front. The enemy will be Islam. Within every Western country there exists a population of Muslims. In the US it is estimated to be over 5 million, England 1.5 million, Germany 3 million and France over 6 million. Within these populations are radicals that will want to join the Jihad. The percentage of these radicals may be less than one percent, however that equates to several thousand in each of the countries listed above. Something will have to be done to 'neutralize' the extremists. Visiting Muslims may be asked to leave some countries and may include students and other classes. But the millions of residents, most being legal citizens of these countries may need a level of protection against acts of revenge. No matter what acts or steps are taken to deal with the millions of Muslims living in these countries it will serve to further divide the populace between Muslim and Christian. This is exactly what Iran would hope for as Muslim nations in the Middle East ponder their choices.

The end to this strategy comes when the West is willing to engage on the frontline. That will come when the casualties mount and the fate of the 'hostages' is no longer in question. When the 'value' of a hostage is reduced to nil, then engagement of troops will occur and the battles will rage in earnest. This is the way of war. But this war will be different from others as ruthless regimes, fighting for their very survival will employ every weapon in their arsenal, including biological and chemical agents. They will be employed on Western soil in Western cities as their homelands become targets. This coming Jihad will be lead by the most desperate of men in an all-or-nothing fight to the finish. But a Jihad cannot be conducted by Iran alone.

Iran may send out the 'Call' for the Jihad, however there needs to be a few other participants for it to reach anything more than a bad week or two. The US and combined Arab Gulf countries can repel most if not all Iranian military actions that may arise in retaliation for being attacked. There are some elements of Iran's activities that will, however, be difficult to control. These include their submarine fleet and their network of activists, both domestic and international that can, if given the opportunity, wreck some havoc. These do not constitute a Jihad but do demand serious attention.

Iraq is the wild card in such a move against Iran. Iran is predominately Shiite and Iraq is the only other nation that has a majority of Shiite Muslims. One question that springs to mind is "How will Iraq react to a major attack by the US against Iran?" Again, assuming that such an attack would result in the loss of thousands of civilians, and there would be calls for humanitarian aid for the plight of at least the women and children, then what do the Shiites of Iraq do? Most of the most powerful Shiite figures and politicians in Iraq have received substantial support from Iran in their time of need and will feel some level of connection and obligation to the Iranians. And Iran has influence with some of the more powerful Shiite groups in Iraq and has given arms, cash training and other support in the past to the Shiites and others. The question of how Iraq will react is not as simple as 'For, Neutral or Against'. There will be a thousand shades of gray from sealing off its border with Iran to Parliament evicting all American troops without their weapons and attacking any that don't. How the Iraqis will react to the US attacking Iran will also be influenced largely by the nature, duration and aftermath of the assault.

The Iranian nuclear program could most probably be set back a number of years with the destruction of half a dozen or less facilities. An attack of this nature with precision munitions would be a clear US message to Iran and the world that the US will not allow an Iranian nuclear program. An attack of this nature might actually come as a relief to other Arab nations in the region that fear the day Iran goes nuclear. This type of attack would lessen Iran's ability to gain international sympathy that could ultimately lead to a Jihad as casualties, particularly civilian casualties could be kept to an absolute minimum. Although Iran could call upon its substantial and increasing network of agents and sympathizers within Iraq, it is doubtful that such an action would inspire the broad base of Shiite population to take up arms on Iran's behalf. However, this type of attack would also leave Iran's military capabilities in full force with the ability to launch attacks against any number of vital targets in the immediate vicinity. Even the US and combined Arab Gulf countries would have difficulty defending all their interests and insure the safe passage of oil through the Strait of Hormuz. And such an attack would not guarantee the destruction of Iran's nuclear capability, only set it back and perhaps slow its future development. An attack on all of the known Iranian facilities related to its nuclear program could exceed two hundred targets and possibly as high as three hundred targets. Such an attack would effectively set their nuclear program back to zero. It could conceivably still be considered as a 'limited' attack restricted only to their nuclear program. However, it would almost certainly raise the Iranian casualties into the high tens of thousands, a large portion being civilian. This would be a dangerous proposition as the more casualties Iran suffers, the more sympathy they can garner. At some point, if Iran feels that the vast majority of international opinion and sympathy is with them, then they might be encouraged to retaliate with all out military action. Leaving the Iranian military largely intact after such an attack would be a very dangerous gamble indeed. Iran wouldn't have to retaliate immediately, but could step up the propaganda war that may tip the balance against the US in Iraq.

An all out attack against the Iranian nuclear program and military might as well include attacks against its infrastructure to facilitate a collapse of the government. Though much of the rural Iranian 'villages' do not rely heavily upon the infrastructure of the nation, most of the cities, industrial complexes and military do. Power, water, communications and the transportation networks are quite vulnerable to anyone that has command of the skies. A sustained attack of these targets would take at least a week and more probably two or three weeks. The first Gulf War began with a seven week air campaign. Thereafter, strikes would be conducted against any target of opportunity that presented itself. It is this continued aggression in the face of a devastated Iran that could be viewed as an attack on Islam. Iranian casualties could easily exceed one hundred thousand and could possibly reach triple that figure. Any further attacks, however militarily prudent, could very well be viewed as excessive. The longer the attacks continued the more agitated the Iraqi Shiites would become. The longer the attacks continued the more agitated Muslims in the Middle East and around the globe would become.

If a US military planner where to be asked how to strike Iran's nuclear program and then defend against any retaliation against the oil interests and passage in the Gulf arena, chances are that he would recommend an all out attack to include military and infrastructure targets. This will be a military action as whatever efforts have been attempted at a political solution seemed to have failed.

Which side actually fires the first volley is almost secondary to the fact that the US will bring the might of its military upon Iran. It is likely that immediately before the hostilities begin there will be some 'new intelligence' about the Iranian nuclear program. Perhaps it will be Israeli intelligence, or an Iranian defector with details of the program or US satellite images that indicate Iran's intentions for developing 'the bomb'. Demands and ultimatums can be leveled at Iran for immediate cessation and full inspection compliance. The Iranians will certainly object and may even fire the first volley. The Iranians may attack a ship, take control of an off shore oil well or position their ships to blockade the Strait of Hormuz. Again, the exact sequence of the events unfolding is not as important as the degree to which the US conducts its campaign against Iran. The characteristics of the US action will dictate how quickly and how many countries join Iran. Syria will join Iran as it knows it is already on the US bad-boy list and nothing short of a regime change will change that. Libya will probably join soon after the hostilities begin. Morocco's participation will be sought by Iran as the Strait of Gibraltar can close the Mediterranean. Most of North Africa will join the Jihad at some point except for Egypt that will try to hold out against the 'Calling'. Again, Turkey will be the key and critical mass necessary for the Jihad to gain momentum and transform the conflict from a local or regional action to a World War status.

A SCENARIO

During the first half of 2011 we can expect to see more 'alarming' reports, findings and warnings from Israel and the US on Iran's nuclear ambitions. More reactors, more and better centrifuges, more uranium being refined until it becomes assumed that Iran wants the capability to produce vast amounts of nuclear weapons or perhaps just wants to provide nuclear generated electricity for the entire Middle East. Reports of Iranian military buildup with cutting edge Russian technology will continue. And accusations and calculations of Iranian nuclear ambitions and capabilities will become more prevalent. These will be in the news for any wishing to heed the warnings. There will also be final military preparations by the US, Israel and others for the ultimate showdown with Iran. Munitions, anti-missile missiles, supplies and reserves of fuel will be stockpiled. US troop rotations will be adjusted to have maximum capability during the second half of 2011. Sometime, during the early Fall of 2011 the 'rhetoric' will take on a more ominous tone. Perhaps challenges to Iran's fledgling space program that demand that it be monitored so Iran does not put up anything more than observational satellites. Fear mongering on their space program has much potential for an orbiting warhead that can be brought down at will means that no city anywhere in the world is beyond Iran's reach. Tel Aviv, London, Washington, Riyadh, Moscow which one will be targeted, or will it be all? An Iran with a weapon orbiting in space would be intolerable no matter what the odds of actually achieving this milestone. The US will probably not confront Iran directly but will continue to press for ever increasing sanctions against the regime. When the US makes a military move against Iran it wants it to be as much as a surprise as possible. This is probably part of the motivation behind the release of the US Intelligence Report citing that Iran has discontinued efforts towards nuclear weapons since 2003. The release of that report helped to diffuse tension between the US and Iran and lessened the need for any immediate military action by either side. At the appropriate time that particular Intelligence Report can be claimed to be intentionally flawed to allow sufficient time for final preparations against Iran and insure the flow of oil out of the Gulf. That 'appropriate time' could be immediately following the onset of a US attack on Iran.

As Israel takes the public lead in anti-Iranian affairs, the US and the Arab Gulf states will continue with their military preparations. Between now and the onset of military action we can expect the diligent reporting in the Western media of every aspect of Iran's nuclear activities. Any improvement in centrifuging, acquiring new materials or processes, any lack or reporting to the IEAE and all threatening rhetoric will be reported as Israel and the US continue to build the nuclear case against Iran. Every Iranian military advancement, acquisition and activity of any consequence will also be reported in the Western media. All the little news 'dots', and there will be many, will strongly suggest that Iran is building nuclear weapons, ballistic and inter-continental missiles and maybe even a satellite delivery system to rain down mushroom clouds over any city or target in the world. Possibly in September there may be a new 'finding' that somewhat 'confirms' that Iran is and has been working diligently on nuclear weapons. A high ranking Iranian defector, satellite pictures or other evidence that confirm the existence of an Iranian nuclear program would enable the US to deliver a harsh and immediate ultimatum to the

Iranians including a warning that any signs of Iranian military mobilization would be deemed an act of war. Hostilities would begin very soon afterwards. Within hours, the US would gain overwhelming air superiority enabling it to begin the systematic destruction of Iran's most dangerous offensive weapons, including aircraft, missiles and navy. In the days that follow Iran's military will all but dissolve. Iran may score a tactical victory or two but for the most part Iran's retaliation efforts in the Gulf will be checked. Iran may even successfully hamper or even 'blockade' the Strait of Hormuz temporarily. At the time of hostilities, if oil flow is still required to be shipped out via the Strait then any blockage or threat will be quickly neutralized by the US. The US military commanders will have the securing the flow of oil as their primary military objective and will focus the phenomenal power of the US military within striking distance to achieve those ends. Again, the lesson learned by the Middle East about not fighting a war on your own home ground will come to bare. That Iran's conventional warfare machinery may be all but decimated does not prevent them from a single act of retaliation far from the theater of war. This would be an act of desperation that had to unify the Muslim population around the world against the US. And again, there is no single 'accessible' structure in the world that compares to the Vatican. The most accessible targets would be in Europe and the most notable, recognizable targets would fall far short in forcing a World War. Big Ben in London or the Eiffel Tower in Paris would pale in comparison to the global impact of the sacking of the Vatican. It would send a message to all Christians that they couldn't even keep their most sacred house of Christianity safe. The sacking of the Vatican would immediately transform the hostilities from a US and Israel verses Iran conflict to a battle between Moslems and Christians the world over. The Iranians would make sure that the new message was heard. Rome, the city that houses the city-state of the Vatican is accessible by sea and is largely undefended. It is certainly militarily vulnerable by a strike force armed with biological or chemical weapons that can secure the major arteries of the city until thousands of reinforcements arrive a few hours later. Such an attack would most probably be launched in the predawn hours during a weekend or holiday. Notices would be given to the US and European governments that if any action is taken against the few hundred securing the city or the few thousand reinforcements on the way then the fate of the couple of million residence of Rome would be sealed. It is even conceivable that once 'biologicals' were in place around the city that Iran could recruit the assistance of the Italians to 'cooperate or else…'. Reaction time is the crucial element in such a scenario and chances are that a small strike force can be in place with their threat of biological or chemical agents before their surprise mission can be detected let alone intercepted. Once in place, the safe passage of reinforcements is somewhat secured as no Western government is prepared to trade off two million of its own population against a few thousand of the enemy. Even if half the 'hostages' escape during the chaos of the initial attack that still leaves one million hostages. When reinforcements arrive and secure the city, the process begins again, capturing city by city along the coast. With Rome being held hostage, there would be a fair chance that the US Congress would be compelled to declare war leaving the President our Commander-In-Chief with dictatorial powers. Before mass evacuations can be organized in Southern Europe and while the threat of one to two million Italian hostages are still in the balance the Jihad has the advantage and could probably establish a second 'beach head' or in this case, capture another large port city. That city would probably be Marseilles in Southern France. It will not be long before Europe, the Middle East and the US are engaged in all out war, primarily around the Mediterranean. The Jihadists goal will be to take control of the Mediterranean islands and coastline in an effort to deny Israel ship traffic. Without shipping, Israel would be on a fast track to a near feudal economy. This tactic also requires more participants in the Jihad other than Iran. Morocco would be instrumental in sealing the Mediterranean and then continue along the Spanish coast. Turkey is the land bridge to Europe and would control the Black Sea/Mediterranean Sea traffic. Additionally, Turkey would be instrumental in attacking Greece and the Aegean Islands. Libya would have easy access to many of the Mediterranean islands including Malta, Sicily, Sardinia and many more. At some point during the campaign the utility of the hostages are lost. That point comes when a sufficient number of them have been killed, tortured or otherwise given up for 'lost'. Once the hurdle of the hostages is overcome then engagement on all fronts happens. Even China will be more than happy to assist in neutralizing the threats from Pakistan and Iran as they make their way to the oil rich Middle East. China can and will employ a two hundred million man army to hue a land path straight to the Middle East in hopes of 'securing' the oil fields. The European coast will be retaken and the Jihad will fail. Last ditch efforts of the Jihad to strike a blow directly at Israel will be the scene of the largest conventional warfare confrontation. Again, the Jihad will fail against the combined military might of the West, Israel and China. Losses of both sides will reach into the millions and many millions more injured or suffering from exposure to some limited use of biological, chemical and nuclear weapons.

This is a scenario that seems highly unlikely yet disturbingly plausible. There is an exceptionally high probability that President Obama will deliver a strike at the Iranian nuclear program should Iran achieve weapons production capability. President Obama doesn't want Iran to produce nuclear weapons. Israel certainly does not want Iran to produce nuclear weapons. Kuwait, Saudi Arabia, the Emirates, Bahrain and Qatar don't really want Iran to have nuclear weapons. Europe doesn't want a nuclear Iran. And President Obama has publicly reference the unacceptable prospect of a nuclear Iran. President Obama will, in all probability, strike Iran's nuclear program before he leaves office.

The reality of totally eliminating Iran's nuclear program pretty much means an all-out assault. To strike all of Iran's nuclear program means targeting over 200 targets and possibly as high as 300 targets. Some of these facilities are large and will require multiple missiles or bombs to ensure their destruction. This suggests that hundreds, if not thousands, of Cruise missiles and/or bomber sorties will be needed to complete the job. Some attention will have to be given to neutralizing Iran's air defense system to allow these attacks to happen. Such an attack would demand some retaliatory action by Iran so it would be highly irresponsible to leave Iran's military intact. Iran, with its current navy, could easily block the Strait of Hormuz, even if they were to sink their own ships in the shallow waters. Iran's navy could come within striking distance of many critical targets requiring 'engagement' before any damage could be done. Most large naval vessels have big guns with several miles range. So, it seems highly likely that when the US strikes Iran's nuclear program facilities, that it also destroys much of Iran's offensive capability. This means Naval vessels, both above and below water, if possible. The surface vessels pose little problems, however, Iran has developed small submarines for the shallow waters of the Gulf that in theory would be harder to detect. The Iranian Air force would certainly be included in a list of targets as they would pose an unacceptable threat to the oil interests in the region. Iran's missiles and missile program as a whole would also be deemed an unacceptable threat as well, so any missile batteries or missile production facilities would probably also be targeted. About the only part of the Iranian military that would not be deemed an immediate threat would be the troops, tanks and artillery. It would be difficult to target every tank and piece of artillery in Iran and would take several months, not days or a couple of weeks. If, at such time Iran amassed tanks and troops near the Iraqi border then they would pose an easy target.

So now we have the highly probably scenario that the US conducts a major strike against Iran's nuclear program, air defenses and much of its offensive military capabilities. At the very least these strikes will take several days and more probably two to three weeks. Unlike the Iraq war, the US will not look to occupy Iran with the possible exception of a few strategic Iranian islands and coastal area near the Strait of Hormuz. During this approximately two weeks does Iran do nothing? No, they will try to hit the targets most valuable to the US, and that is the Gulf oil. What Iranian missiles that do get launched will test the anti-missile defensive capabilities of the US and Gulf countries. Some missiles will probably hit their targets but damage will most probably be limited and repairable. The Iranian Air Force is no match for the US capabilities that are already employed in the region. It is doubtful that any Iranian jets that make it off the ground to engage the US aircraft will do anything more than to delay the US completing its objectives by more than a few hours. Even Iranian shipping through the Strait will have to be halted for fear of blockage. Three or four good size ships sunk at a critical place could block the passage of heavily laden oil tankers through the Strait. The US will dominate the conventional warfare engagements with Iran. Even Iran's submarines will be vulnerable to attack if they do anything except lie silent. Any torpedo attacks from Iranian submarines would almost certainly spell their demise. Iran will have to try unconventional tactics if it is to strike any blow against the West. The questions then become what kind of unconventional attack and where?

The Gulf will be a beehive of military activity controlled by the US. Every ship on the Gulf will be allowed passage only with the US naval permission. Every ship that moves in the Gulf will be friendly to the US. Iran's move will not be in the Gulf. And be sure that any Iranian troop buildup or border crossing with Iraq will be halted at the earliest possible stage. Iran's move will not happen along the Iraqi border. Iran could pour troops and tanks into Turkey but it better be by invitation as the Turks have formidable armed forces let alone have been very cooperative with the US in the past. It is conceivable that Iran could enter Turkey but with a plea to the population to join the Jihad. Such a move could be successful in getting Turkey to join the Jihad depending upon the circumstances of the day. And Iran invading Turkey would not have the immediate impact needed to transform the US/Iran war to something much larger. Iran could not mount an assault on the US mainland for logistic and exposure prohibit it. Iran has few allies.

Even during and after the US assault on Iran as Iran tries to sway anti-US opinion few countries will step up publicly in support of Iran. There is Syria but that would only give Iran access to Israel, if Iran can move troops and equipment in vast quantities. And, to attack Israel directly would invite the possible use of nuclear weapons. Libya will probably be in support of Iran but perhaps not publicly. Libya's participation or cooperation would be all that would be required to take the war up to the next level.

Perhaps the most dangerous scenario could be that Iran sees the unmistakable buildup to a US strike against Iran and decides that it must strike first. The Southern European coast offers a target rich environment of largely undefended cities. One of the closest major cities to Libya and the most notable would be Rome, home of the Vatican. A submarine/hovercraft attack force could certainly surprise the city and hold it hostage while reinforcements could arrive. Rome meets all the criteria to transform the basically two-sided regional war to one of global proportions. Rome and the Vatican are accessible, mostly unprotected and would divide Moslems and Christians the world over. If Iran were only capable of a single strike against the West that had to rally Moslems worldwide to a Jihad it would be by taking the city of Rome hostage. During the days immediately following that capture of Rome, both the Moslem world and the Christian world would be turned upside down. For the Christian world, it would be the final straw that would mean it is time to put an end to radical Islam. For much of the Moslem world that has felt that the US is already waging a war on Islam it would be the time to get off the fence. And with the prospects of Europe and the US in an all out war against Islam then they would have little option but to side with the Jihad. The vast majority of Moslems seem to think that their religion is already being held hostage by extremists. When Rome falls then all reasonable voices on both sides will be silenced. Such a 'First Strike' would launch the planet into World War III with an intact and mobilized Iranian military. Having Rome hostage would enable Iran to prepare for action in the Gulf or at the very least mobilize its forces and move them into Turkey, Pakistan or other areas before engaging the US.

THE SIGNS

There will be signs before the next hostilities erupt. And there will be further signs as the hostilities escalate. Some signs will be front page, some signs will be subtle and some may be very difficult to monitor. Taken collectively these indicators will progress to a higher probability of war, if not to a certainty. There are also timeline considerations as Israel, Iran and the Obama administration race towards their preparations.

During the first Gulf War, Saddam had lined up 60 kilometers of tanks, armored vehicles and trucks on the highway beginning at the Kuwaiti border more than two weeks prior to the invasion of Kuwait. Saddam also had two reconnaissance groups take up positions on the two main Islands off the Kuwaiti mainland. Both these facts were reported in a London based Iraqi resistance paper over two weeks prior to the invasion. In this case the signs of war were clear as to the timing, nature and scope of the attack but the warnings fell upon deaf ears as the US Administration wanted to engage Saddam. Prior to the second Iraq war, there was a small article in the 'Emirates Today' online about the growing problem of what to do with the hundreds of crewmen from the growing number of ships that were impounded. These ships had been smuggling out Saddam's oil outside of the UN governed oil trade. Saddam had been smuggling additional oil sales outside of UN monitoring for years and the US had always turned a blind eye. Then, the US began enforcing the restrictions just prior to the second war and began impounding all the ships smuggling Saddam's oil. This action had the consequence of hundreds of desperate, stranded sailors in the Emirates. These sailors had no money as their shipping companies abandoned them placing the problem of their growing number in the lap of the Emirates. A small indicator, but an indicator none the less.

Many of the signs of the coming Jihad, subtle as they may be should be obtainable from 'the Web'. However, what has transpired in the past is no assurance that the sources will continue to be available in the future. In preparing this writing, many 'pages' and indeed whole 'sites' that prompted and inspired this writing have 'disappeared' from the web and indeed, practical history. The 'Web' has no accessible official historical archives of what pages were posted, when and where. It is unfortunate, but one can assume that more of the same will transpire as the powers that be, race towards all out war as a means to settle their differences.

The following signs are not meant to be 'secret revelations' or any other type of sensitive information that both sides of the coming conflict don't already know. Access to these signs will vary in difficulty but certainly are not a security issue on either side. They are meant as early warning signals for the public at large, to enable people to make better informed judgments in choosing their own coarse of preparations in a more timely manner. It is highly unlikely that either side in the coming conflict will share their plans with the general public in any meaningful way.

Before a US strike against Iran's nuclear program can happen, a vast amount of preparation and coordination must transpire amongst several thousand key players. This will lead to a few tens of thousands of non-US military individuals that will have prior knowledge of the attack. Some of these 'thousands' will know just hours or days before the actual attack, some know now. There may be hundreds of people that know all the pertinent details prior to the coming action and others that only glean a single but crucial element of the complex action to take place.

Certainly the Kings, Sheiks and other Middle East leaders that have cooperated extensively with the US on checking Iran's ambitions will be informed. Some of these countries have already been engaged in an effort of re-routing their oil to by-pass the Strait of Hormuz. These Arab countries, whose support and coordination are instrumental in the success of such an action, are ruled by close knit families. Each ruling King or Sheik has their brothers, sons, cousins, uncles and nephews overseeing critical elements of their government and military. Some countries have cliques of ruling families that oversee all government affairs. Saudi Arabia has a ruling family with over 2,000 members of the 'Aristocracy'. It also has a class of 'Super-Merchants' that help facilitate the ruling family's commercial activity. Both these classes are dependent upon the elite 'Technocrats' that keep the country functioning. But the question is not really about how many people in Saudi Arabia or these other countries will have prior knowledge as to the timing of the attack. Rather, the question is, as a result of their prior knowledge, will their individual actions, taken collectively, generate some sign or indication as to 'when' the attack will happen. Will they move their families to the 'West' or other safe havens? Will they buy billions of dollars worth of gold, silver, platinum and diamonds as a hedge? Will they take massive positions in the oil futures market? The answer is 'yes', they will. There are many others who's participation in the massive logistical preparations required will also give an indication. Some of these participants are individuals, some are public corporations. The signs can be loosely categorized in several topics such as politics, religion, the media, military and business.

Indicators can be subtle like an unexplained jump in the volume and price of oil and gold and their futures. There are always people in the know that are just too greedy to pass up the opportunity to make a bit more money. Some signs are calculable and lend themselves to 'higher probability' times such as the deployment of aircraft carrier fleets and the supply ships that service them. There is a higher probability for sustained military action earlier rather than later in a fleet's deployment. Deployment of large service vessels can extend or change the time frame. Much of this information is available on the web and even the withdrawal of the information's availability can be taken as a prelude to some sort of activity. Awarding of certain military contracts that seemingly suggest high inventories of certain consumables used during conflicts.

Though the coming Jihad will be waged upon religious differences, it has its origins in the political arena. So we begin with the political signs.

The political signs will be a rich environment, most of which will be subject to debate. But here we are not looking for debate, rather any indication of new or shifting alliances. The most important signs to watch for would probably be in Turkey. Iran on its own could remain isolated and contained, however, with Turkey joining, the Jihad would take a quantum leap with the potential of opening up four new fronts, three of which are in the back door of Europe. There are two Turkeys, one, the large military complex that makes up NATO's second largest army (second only to the US) and the elected government of the 70+ million populace. The Turkish military has many close and guarded ties with the US military and administration. Turkey has been an invaluable asset to the US all during the Cold War with major radar and listening stations directed towards the Soviet Union and as a 'gate-keeper' between the Soviet fleet in the Black Sea and the Mediterranean Sea. More recently, Turkey has cooperated with the US on troop and supply movement in the US's Iraq campaigns. The Turkish military has also cooperated with the US with pro-Israeli activities, a point of contention in much of the Middle East. The Turkish military does not run the country, rather they have 'allowed' the elected government to run the country provided that its policies and decisions do not conflict with the military agenda. However, the population of Turkey is overwhelmingly Muslim and, in recent years have been using the political electoral process to gain control of the Parliament. The increasingly pro-Islamic government have been instituting gradual change to a more Islamic friendly State. Gradually, brick by brick, the walls that had kept Islam out of government are being torn down. Some changes may seem insignificant by Western standards like allowing Muslim women attending Universities to have the right to wear a 'Hijab', the head coverings prescribed by Islam. By comparison, if a female university student in any Western society were to be prohibited from wearing a cross around her neck then there would be an uproar of injustice. But the Turkish rendition has a far deeper implication of separation of religion and state. The wearing of head scarves by female university attendees, now allowed by Turkish Parliament, is a sign that Islam can no longer be made subservient to the 'secular' Turkish society of the past. It is now a visual reminder to the would-be intelligentsia of the country that a new era is emerging, one in which you can be Muslim first and still partake in all the opportunities the state has to offer. The secular society of Turkey has been put on notice. Though many of these small signs of growing Islamic influence may become apparent, it is their collective impact that indicates that an Islamic population is moving towards dominant political action through a representative Parliament. The real challenge that warrants monitoring is the Parliamentary challenges to the Turkish military, particularly on issues that divide Islam and the US. The struggle between the Turkish military and their Parliament will continue and be a valuable source of indicators to the level of Muslim influence in national affairs. Every instance of the military yielding power to the will of the masses is a declaration of the growing dominance of Islam in Turkey. This is the key point in assessing when (not if) Turkey will be ripe to join an Iranian instigated Jihad. Turkey is systematically becoming more pro-Islamic and at some point it's generals, colonels and majors will have to side with their brothers, fathers, sons, uncles, cousins and nephews that reside in the population at large.

Turkey has several English web sites for news and reports. One must understand that all official reporting sites should be taken with a large dose of salt. That being said, these sites are still a good source for internal affairs and gauging the increase of Islam in government affairs.

Next to Turkey, any of the North African Arab countries would be a boon to an Iranian called Jihad. It is very doubtful that the pro-US government of Egypt would comply as the US ties and influence within the Egyptian military extends through most of its top officers. Even when much of the populace of Egypt may want to join a Jihad, the military will be very slow to sever or even test the relationship with their US sponsors. It is the other North African States that would be worth monitoring for signs of Iranian ties, Islamic Jihadist increase or increasing anti-US stance. These countries are Libya, Tunisia, Algeria and Morocco. Any one of these countries would add tactical and strategic value in the Mediterranean Basin.

In the case of Morocco, the Strait of Gibraltar would be compromised. This would allow only 'Jihad friendly' ship traffic through the Strait while denying all other traffic, effectively putting enormous constraints on any Western fleets operating in the basin and essentially putting them on the clock. These constraints would be both operational and time wise as any fleet operations require huge amounts of resupply and refueling, particularly in time of war. In the case of Tunisia, its proximity to Sicily, Italy and other islands make it the ideal launch point for initial strikes, particularly with existing ferry routes. Libya and Algeria would give hundreds of miles of coastline that could be used as launch sites that would be difficult to defend against. In the case of Libya, its leader would not need much prompting and Algeria has about five million people in France many of which are treated as second class citizens.

It is a fair statement the radical Islam has been on the increase across North Africa, the Middle East and Southern Asia for the past few years. In some places the authorities have checked any public expression of this increase. However, the increase is real and continues to grow. It seems that radical Islam would be the natural ally of an Iranian instigated Jihad. This is a powder keg waiting for the fuse to be lit. Igniting this fuse can be anything from a simple insult to Islam to the killing of a prominent religious or political figure. The Abu Garab prison scandal did more for the recruiting of anti-American activists than most other recruiting efforts combined. When the US strikes a blow at the Iranian nuclear program, there may be mosques that are destroyed, and possibly schools with children and undoubtedly scores of innocent bystanders, plenty of material for the propaganda wars that follow a strike. Before the strike, watch for increasing pressure on radical Islamic groups in these countries.

Most of the rest of the Arab world has already chosen sides with the Arab Gulf States behind the US and Syria tied to Iran. Jordan has and will continue to support the US privately, so long as King Abdullah reigns. Lebanon is still trying to consolidate its government and would prefer to sit out any further conflicts. However, there are strong forces at work in Lebanon with direct ties to the militant Palestinian groups, Syria and Iran.

Iraq has had enough of war, occupation and outside influences and efforts continue to reduce or eliminate the radical elements such as Al Sadr's Mehdi army. Iraq can be a great strategic advantage for the US or an anchor around its neck. If the pro-Iranian elements in Iraq are subdued or otherwise neutralized then there still remains the powerful Shiite groups that have a majority in parliament. The largest and most powerful group, headed by the Hakim family, owes much to Iran. Iraq could rise up in arms against the US and make any US operations in Iraq ineffectual. However, in the aftermath of a US attack on Iran, Iraq may be able to trade its genuine freedom from US occupation for Iraq's indifference to the conflict, a tempting possibility for Iraq. In Iraq the stakes for the Iraqis, the US and Iran are exceptionally high. The US troops in Iraq would definitely be a target for some sort of retaliatory action by Iran and are increasingly being targeted by the same. Having the US military poised along the Iranian border poses a threat that could strike freely at almost any target in Iran. That is, provided the Iraqis do not hinder US operations. Although the US could institute the most severe Marshal Law in Iraq, it would detract measurably from US military assets that could be employed against Iran. It would be far more advantageous for the US to have the Iraqis cooperate and at the very least remain neutral. This cooperation may come at a high political cost. Iran would look at Iraq as an opportunity to wage war on the US and not on Iranian soil. Iran would exercise every avenue open to them to arm every pro-Iranian and anti-US groups within Iraq. The US would have to close virtually all of Iraq's borders to prevent arms and fighters crossing in to Iraq from Iran, Syria, Saudi Arabia, and possibly with Jordan and Turkey as well. Trade would be bottlenecked at the few crossings that could be controlled or just totally prohibited. For the existing Iranian backed anti-US networks in Iraq, Iran would call upon them to wreck as much havoc as possible.

Aside from the Middle East, there should be political signs with other countries. The US interacts with Europe, Russia and China on any number of issues on any given day and preparations for something as significant as a major US strike against Iran's nuclear program would not go undetected by their respective intelligence agencies.
Europe, as a whole, seems to be far more subtle and adept at political affairs than the US. This makes monitoring their affairs all the more difficult. Tracking the movements and meetings of European officials and dignitaries can yield some possible clues, however, many European countries will have their own internal potential problems when the US prepares to strike Iran. France, England and Germany each have significant Moslem populations. France has their Algerians from the colonial days. England has Pakistanis and other Moslems that have spilled over from their Commonwealth. And Germany has their Turkish population, brought in as cheap labor in the years before the German East/West unification. If Europe was to exhibit any political signs of preparing for a US strike on Iran perhaps the most visible would be on monitoring and perhaps preparing to clamp down on any radical segments within their Moslem communities.

At first glance one might assume that the Russians would be dead set against such an action. Russia has multi-billion dollars in sales to Iran of military hardware and technology. Russia is building the Iranian nuclear reactor and continues to support Iran in the UN by vetoing most of the punitive measures that the US wants to impose upon Iran. By somewhat empowering Iran, Russia has raised the level of instability in the region and helped make Iran a possible threat to Israel. But Russia has profited greatly from this instability in the past by far more than the military and other sales to Iran. Russia is a major oil and gas exporter, an industry exceptionally near and dear to Putin's heart. The $20 to $50 of 'instability and speculation' that is now built into the price of a barrel of crude oil means that Putin's 'very close friends' that run the Russian oil industry have gained tens of billions of dollars over the past few years. A US strike on Iran would also include some sort of blockading of Iranian oil exports and the Iranian threat of closing the Strait of Hormuz and could easily send the spot price of crude to two or three hundred dollars a barrel or even higher if the Strait does indeed close or Iran scores a few hits on Gulf oil instalations. Though Russia may be compelled to publically thwart US ambitions against Iran, it will be Russia that profits, perhaps the most from any US strike against Iran. The economic clues will be more difficult to detect this time around as compared to past conflicts. 'Hedging' has almost become an institution as savvy investors, hedge funds and mutual funds desperately try to second guess the impact of world events on trading futures. The trading volume of today's precious metal markets and oil futures has risen as of late, however, with careful tracking and analysis could yield clues as to when substantial new money enters the market. Gold, and other precious metals have traditionally been the ultimate hedge against the perils of war. But this war will have the greatest impact on the price of oil. Oil and the precious metals are already trading near all time highs and may dissuade potential investors to the real up-side potential. There are no limits in the territory that is about to be charted. Yet, there will be a tremendous increase in demand for these as war approaches. The real investment danger in oil is that it will be 'commandeered' and rationed worldwide. Strategic reserve or not, if the oil supplies from the Gulf are interrupted while the US is waging another military action, then it would be really difficult for the US administration not to impose some sort of controls over the oil supply and distribution. This would not be the case for precious metals. Gold in particular should see a somewhat steady rise from now until the time the US strikes Iran. Even during price pullbacks as all traded metals do, there should be a trend that indicates that there is a fundamental growth in demand particularly on the futures around or close after a presumed attack date. Prices may fluctuate with speculators reacting to positive and negative news, however, as we approach closer to military action there should be increasing underlying demand reflected in the prices.

Another economic signal may be the purchase of high profile luxury property in the West by the more prominent Arabs. Arab investment in publically traded companies should also increase significantly though sometimes difficult to monitor.

Military signs are a sensitive subject as it is the core of the subject matter and the only required element for the strike. Obviously, there is little chance that the US would begin a campaign if all its carriers were at dockside in the US. But there are other signals that one may use as early indicators. Escalations in challenging situations are a ready indicator and can easily erupt into large scale violence. This includes activity such as when Iranian speed boats harass the larger shipping vessels passing through the Strait. Although it is meant as a show of capability by Iran as to the vulnerability of the Strait, this kind of action can easily escalate. One craft comes too close and gets fired upon, then fire is returned, then more shots fired. Or escalating events can be of the nature similar to when Iran seized a British craft with a few crew members and held them in Iran for trespassing into their territorial waters. Next time there might be a bit more resistance. One shot fired, one casualty in such an incident could quickly erupt into something much larger. So long as Iran and the US are challenging each other publically and privately, then there will continue to be plenty of opportunities for explosive military situations. Even the mobilization of one sides troops or military exercises can be misinterpreted and lead to escalation and engagement.

The "X" factor, x being an unknown or unquantifiable factor will most probably be responsible for the beginning of military engagements. This can take several forms, all of which will come 'as a surprise' to the general public. Taking the time frame considerations of the US with its presidential election and Israel's pressing desire to eliminate the Iranian threat yesterday, the X factor will probably surface once the US has made all its military preparations. One possible X factor would be satellite intelligence that 'confirms' that the Iranians are indeed working on nuclear weapons and close to production capability. This may even involve revealing monitoring technologies that have been classified secret. Another possible X factor would be the defection of a high ranking Iranian official that 'testifies' that the Iranians have an advanced nuclear weapons program or his stolen laptop reveals the same. Such testimony, made public, would justify immediate ultimatums issued by the US for Iran to cease all activity and to allow immediate access to any and all suspected sites with the understanding that any Iranian military mobilization would be deemed an act of war. The X factor may even originate from a third party such as Russia, Pakistan or North Korea that claims that the Iranians are sidetracking nuclear fuel for nuclear weapons. Whatever the X factor turns out to be, it will be accompanied with an immediate call to arms with the US strike against the Iranian nuclear program happening within days. Traditional buildup of rhetoric will just not suffice in today's political climate. There will be a clear and present danger that is validated to the satisfaction of the majority of the US public at that particular point in time. Then, any military strike and subsequent actions will have the backing of the American public, an all important factor during a time close to the US elections. If the initial US military campaign is successful in eliminating Iran's nuclear weapons program and prevent the Iranians from disrupting the flow of oil, then this creates a totally different landscape for any elections. A world in which a continued US military intervention was required for the continued flow of oil would presumably create a political climate favorable to where a diehard military man would qualify as a candidate for president. And any talk of 'opening up a dialogue' with the enemy during the height of the military engagements would be political suicide.

No matter what form the 'X Factor' takes the important point is that it will come. It will come at the most convenient time in regards to reaction. Perhaps on a Friday evening, when the markets are closed for the weekend and most of America is asleep. And, if by Monday morning it is evident that the US has total domination of the skies and sea then the negative effects of the war on the economy might be minimized. Even if it is an act of aggression by Iran that escalates that begins the war, the war will begin and begin in the Gulf.

The movement of political leaders can give an indication of an approaching storm. Although not a requirement political leaders often meet face to face prior to the onset of a major military campaign. The Middle East has been a beehive of activity for the leaders recently but there should be some sort of 'last go around' prior to the launch of the campaign. There might not be any significant signs made public before pre-emptive action is taken or an ultimatum given. Regardless of the signs the storm approaches. Israel's land-grab policy and mistreatment of the Palestinians, the Palestinian's use of missiles and popularizing suicide bombers, America's blind support and protection of Israel, Iran's outdated religious extremism, all after decades of heavy propaganda by both sides of the Arab/Israeli issue means that the war is inevitable. Oil, religious divides, vulnerabilities on both sides and other factors suggest that any Jihad that gains enough traction to move into the Mediterranean theater means millions of casualties on both sides. It also means that there can be no fence-sitters. All of Southern Europe, the Mediterranean Sea and the entire Middle East will be the theater for the conventional warfare engagements with support from America, the rest of Europe, Russia, China, Pakistan and many others fully engaged. As Iran turns on its nuclear reactor the world waits with baited breath for the next step. It will not have to wait long for the coming Jihad.

CONCLUSION

Future events may or may not unfold along the scenario I have put forth. There may be some slight deviation or even a major event unforeseen or unspoken of here. However, as of today, this is what I've come to believe. I've come to believe this because there are a few truths about world affairs that together I just think spell World War III. Israel is not really going to give up land! They may act like they are going to and even say that they will but they will not. Radical Islam doesn't think that it is radical but just correct and everyone else including over 900 million other Moslems are just incorrect or infidels awaiting enlightenment. For whatever reason Iran is now the enemy of the US and Israel. Much of the rest of the West and even the Middle East regimes are now scared of Iran's nuclear ambitions as indeed they should be. If Iran is allowed to develop nuclear arms production, let alone nuclear arms mass production then Israel looses, game over for Israel. If that is allowed to happen then Iran will gain, first the hearts of the vast majority of the Arab world, then their oil. So, that will not be allowed to happen. Why? Because Israel can, on its own, start World War III all by itself just by attacking Iran. But the US can certainly demilitarize Iran and most probably 'safeguard' its allies regimes in the Middle East and even have a notable chance for containment of war. But Iran knows this and when it sees the inevitable 'writing on the wall' then it could very well strike first. Pre-emptive attack or retaliation by whom between the US and Iran doesn't matter too much as Turkey is all too swiftly moving towards their Moslem brothers and away from their military enforced secular status. One 'X' factor (unseen event) could easily galvanize Turkey overnight into an anti-West/pro-Islamic nation. That almost happened when the Turkish 'aid ship' to break the embargo of Gaza was boarded by Israeli commandoes resulting in the deaths of a few Turkish members on board. The Turkish political shift away from the military control that has quietly enforced all Turkey's important foreign policy has already appeared to be under the pursuit of Islamic beliefs and goals. This is very convenient for the Turkish politicians as it affords them a measure of protection from the military and it is also very convenient for the Iranian regime that are trying to propagandize their trying to champion the Islamic causes. Turkey and Iran are neighbors and the Turkish military would have to think thrice if they wanted to eject their pro-Islamic government that has the votes of the majority of their populace if that government had the full support and backing of the Iranian regime. It's just the nature of the changing politics of the neighborhood. Turkey and Iran together on anything spells trouble. 'Containment' of any sorts becomes wishful thinking and Turkey may even be able to intercede on behalf of the Iranians and stall any imminent US strike on Iran. Turkey and Iran are moving closer together so I still see World War III on the horizon.

Most of the preceding has been based upon some historical and present events and my interpretation and extrapolation towards a future outcome, event or point in the future. This leaves room for a tremendous margin of error as 'events' have a habit of happening to the surprise of most, unless…, unless there is a destiny, a pre-ordained future, as it is written. Cause and effect, any physicist will tell you this happened because that happened and made it happen and I am a firm believer that everything that has transpired dictates what will transpire. That we do not know what all the 'factors' are that govern events, particularly 'man-made event' does not mean to say that they are still nothing more than the summation of all preceding events, activities, forces etc.etc. A simple illustration would be a deck of 52 cards. If this is your 'known universe' they you can deduce many things from the unfolding of a deck. Some things you can calculate odds of happening and some things you can calculate certainties. For example, if you have turned over twenty six red cards then you 'KNOW' that the next twenty six will all be black cards, simple enough if you know your 'universe'. The vast majority of us does not know our universe and haven't got a clue as to the complexities of human activities and interactions. Yet I believe that if we 'KNEW EXACTLY' a person's biology, chemistry and everything about him, everything, meaning every neuron in his brain, what was implanted in each, an exact map of the dendrites (connections amongst the neurons) and how each was 'weighed-in' in the thought process, then I believe we could predict with certainty the response of that individual to any situation. We should be able to 'calculate exact words they who say to a given situation even exact physical reactions. That we are miles away from such knowledge of the 'ultimate deck of cards' does not mean that destiny isn't written, it just means that we are only just a few thousand years from grunting at each other and still have a lot to learn. Yet, throughout time, there have been some that have glimpsed the future. Most of those that have glimpsed the future have 'seen' something that has pertained directly to them or their loved ones, not earth shaking events. And there are those very few that have filled pages of our future. Some prophets have filled the pages of the now blurred Bible and others. Undeniably Nostradamus, Malachy, even Edgar Cayce have all 'seen' the future, so for the very few the future is seeable. And if the future is seeable by the very few then perhaps it's not by happenstance that we find ourselves on the brink of World War III but by destiny. Perhaps Ronald Reagan found out after taking office that the Iranians were indeed going to be the crux of World War III so he reneged on his private deals with them. Perhaps successive Presidents found out the same thing and continued an anti-Iranian policy.

I do remember a conversation with Uri Gellar, an individual that has some extraordinary powers. He is extremely telepathic and has a strong magnetic field, perhaps ten times stronger than the weak magnetic field of the earth. He made my watch advance 30 minutes and one of my spoons bend while only touching the fingers of my daughter who was actually holding the spoon. Uri had told me that he had been tested by the 'Americans' and the 'Russians' and that (and I quote) "I (Uri) was nothing compared to what the Americans had and that they were nothing compared to what the Russians had". I can see why having even just glimpses of the future by psychics would be of tremendous value and of the utmost national security interest. So perhaps there is a destiny that explains some seemingly irrational behavior in the global political arena.

I do know that we are drawing near to a ferocious battle between the Iranian regime and all the extremists it can muster against the West. For whatever reasons the West has seen fit to treat Iran as an enemy since the fall of the Shah. The reasons no longer matter as the West imposed sanctions have forced Iran to develop much of its military capability in-house and now it seeks nuclear weapons. A Jihad is in the making just waiting for a catalyst or spark of some kind.

How long before Iran manufactures a nuclear bomb? Two bombs? Or twenty bombs? The war is coming soon and Iran will have to try to force Moslems against Christians for its very survival as we have left it no other choice.

I pray that I am wrong.